FOUNDATIONS

OF

GLORY

BRUCE D. ALLEN

Books by Bruce D. Allen

Gazing into Glory

Promise of the Third Day

The Prophetic Promise of the Seventh Day

Translation by Faith

FOUNDATIONS

OF

GLORY

Living Everyday
In the Heavenly Realm

STILL WATERS INTERNATIONAL MINISTRIES

ISBN 13- 978-0-9978572-9-0

ISBN 10-0997857293

Dedication

This book is dedicated to all those who are passionate to walk in their inheritance as sons of God. To those who are willing to take steps of faith and believe God is no respecter of persons but will give them everything the Word says belongs to them, I say, "Be it done unto you according to your faith!" You will soon see that the Lord desires for you to have everything He paid for you to have. He will help you and guide you on this journey! God will richly bless you!

Acknowledgements

Writing a book is not an easy task, at least not for me. It takes time, energy, and experience to be able to communicate a message from the heart of God. I learned many years ago that if I have not received and walked in the revelation I try to share then at best I am only presenting a possibility or theory.

In this book, I bring to you revelation that I have been slowly walking out for the last seven years since my last book, Gazing Into Glory. I will be the first to admit I have not arrived; rather, I've begun a journey of discovery into untold realms of intimacy with our Lord.

It is with this in mind that I want to thank my best friend and my heart, my wife Reshma, for walking with me and standing by me through this season of discovery. Were it not for her encouragement and strength, I may not have come to this point at this time and most likely ever.

I want to thank so many who have been an inspiration and are a part of my life in this adventure in God! Eternity alone will unveil the full impact each of you have played in the making and molding of who I am becoming in Christ. Thank you!

Endorsements

I would like to acknowledge Bruce Allen as a dear friend and brother in Christ. He's been a dedicated scholar of the Word of God for over 45 years. Bruce travels all over the world to train and disciple believers in preparation for these end times. This book is greatly influenced by the Holy Spirit to bring new insights in the realm of the supernatural. As a believer who longs to walk with Jesus face to face, I find this book to bring great encouragement, instruction, and hope. Intimacy with Christ takes on new horizons as we realize we were created in His very likeness. There are no limits with God, nor are there any limits with us if we dare to believe.

Christ in us, the hope of glory!

Pastor Melinda Sweet
Shekinah Worship Center

I have known and ministered with Dr. Bruce Allen for the last few years and have come to know him as a man of integrity who wants the very best for this end-time Church. Bruce has the ability to de-mystify the deeper things of God. There is no end of Christian books out there; however, there are not many that deal with the days in which we are living and how we can move on into a new day and a new dynamic walk with the Lord Jesus. This is one such book; however, it requires of us a New Wineskin. We are now living in the end times, and if we are to move on into what God has for this new generation we must go beyond the status quo. There are increasing numbers of Christians today who are beginning to have "Enoch"-like experiences, pushing the boundaries and experiencing a new and dynamic walk with the Lord. The book you hold in your hand is an adventure that has been reserved for the times you are now living in. If you want to move on to a new level in your walk with the Lord Jesus, I highly recommend this book to you as a must-read.

Neville Johnson
The Academy of Light
Australia

Although Foundations of Glory is full of supernatural encounters, this book strongly encourages its readers to focus less on someone's gifting and experiences and look to their character and the fruit, which is far more important. The goal is Christlikeness! At the same time, this book is a challenge to step out and answer the call to become one of the sons of God all of creation has been longing and waiting for.

Dr. David White
Lead Pastor, The Gathering Church
Moravian Falls, North Carolina

Are you hungry to grow in your intimate relationship with the Lord? Do you want to see more of the glory of God? Then this new book, Foundations of Glory, by my good friend Bruce Allen shares just what you need to stir you up and take you to higher levels. Bruce loves to tweak and provoke us in our relationship with the Lord. Bruce has a passion for the glory of God. You will see how light overwhelms the darkness. Bruce also brings clarity by explaining the Hebrew understanding of words. As you read, you will see better in the spirit realm. You will be blessed!

Pastor Barry Hill
Living Stone Church
Spokane, Washington
Now retired after 18 years as lead pastor

Deep revelatory truths can come only through a vessel that has been molded and chiseled in heavenly fire! Dr. Bruce Allen is such a man exhibiting the very character of Christ. Bruce has taken age-old biblical mysteries that the ancients once walked in and redefined them for our last-days generation. These present-day truths, if humbly applied, will cause you to walk as a manifest son of God!

Flo Ellers
End Time Handmaiden, Alaska

I must begin by saying thank you Jesus for releasing this timely revelation to the Bride. I feel a big yes and amen in my spirit. As I have pastored for over 30 years now, I have had countless people give me books they tell me I must read. I must be honest with you—I have read maybe a total of five.

You might ask, "Why?" Well, it is simple—I only read what Holy Spirit says will add to my purpose and destiny. All the fluff and information in most books doesn't feed my soul; it actually hinders me from going higher. The second reason is I don't know the person writing the book and I am all for character.

I can honestly say I know Bruce, not just as a person but by the Spirit I know his passion, his walk, and his love for Jesus. What comes out of him is what the Lord has put into him, like Paul said to the church of Corinth: "For I received from the Lord that which I also delivered to you" (1 Cor. 11:23). Not what was learned by a man, but by the Lord Himself.

Remember, Paul was not at the last supper, but somehow he had a revelation greater than those who were there. Why? He received it from the Lord.

That is why this book is so important—it is received of the Lord, for those who are the Lord's. As you read, listen deeply to Holy Spirit; He will reveal to you the greater purpose He has for you as an individual, how to walk the walk and not just have the talk. You can and will be impacted for the rest of your life

Pastor Reg Smith
Christ Family Fellowship
Edmonton Alberta

We first met Bruce Allen during a lunch break in Singapore, which proved to be beneficial for my wife,

Stella, and myself. It has been such an encouragement to know that in this modern-day Christian living, one can be translated (translocated) for the purposes of the Gospel of the Kingdom just like Philip in the Bible.

This book helps the reader to focus correctly and zero in on the vital ways to enter into the realms of the Spirit as different individuals are allowed to experience.

Because of Bruce's passion for all Christians to experience the Kingdom life available to them, he has endlessly pursued the Lord and is now conducting Schools of Translation in many parts of the world.

No one I know of has ever embarked on a ministry with this focus like he has.

After he conducted a School of Translation at our church, I saw a sharp rise in our congregation experiencing a deeper walk with the Lord with tangible evidence of having been with the Lord.

This experience was the catalyst and the breakthrough people were searching for, and this book, Foundations of Glory, definitely points you in that direction.

As you read this book and seek the reality of the Kingdom life—as you read and follow the instructions—don't be surprised when you enter that realm of glory!

If this is the first time you've heard about such experiences, then pay attention to the Scriptures, be open to believe, and you will receive.

As you read through the book, come with a teachable heart

and set aside any preconceived ideas you may have. Allow the Word and the Spirit to lead you and teach you.

We appreciate that Bruce has been obedient to God's calling in his life in getting this book printed.

May all the readers be blessed!

Yours in Christ,

Pastor Jose Roco
Sydney, Australia

Foundations of Glory by Bruce D. Allen is a must-read for anyone hungry for the fullness of the Lord, longing to grow in their understanding of who they are in Christ Jesus and their experience of the inexhaustible realms of glory in the invisible Kingdom of God, which our heavenly Father has lovingly laid up for us.

As a prophet and a forerunner of the "Elijah and Enoch generation" God is releasing into the earth, with a mandate from the Lord to "Prepare the way of the Lord," Bruce—through this book, in a loving yet divinely provocative way and with solid biblical teaching, a sharpened eye for true prophetic activity and revelation in our day, and with correlating personal supernatural experiences in God—spurs us all to head on for the perfection that is part of our godly inheritance.

One sign of a great teacher is that he not only walks the path of revelation but is also adept at imparting that revelation to others so they can understand and walk therein also.

Bruce does just that rather graciously in this book. I am particularly enthralled by the depths of his revelation on "light" and the new understanding Bruce brings to the eternal command to "Arise, shine, for thy light is come, and the glory of the Lord is risen upon thee" (Isa. 60:1 KJV).

Our heavenly Father desires for us a supernatural lifestyle as our norm as we lay our lives down for the King. To that end I fully endorse Bruce's new book, Foundations of Glory, and as you read it may you be drawn into the Father's heart until you are so undone that you experience Heaven on earth. Thank you, my friend, for your obedience in conveying and imparting these truths, which many of us long to walk in.

Pastor Michael N Baako
Tabernacle of David Worship Center
Laurel, Maryland

CONTENTS

Revelation, an Open Door 1

The Destiny of God 15

Covenants 23

The Character of Christ 37

Taking Steps of Faith 71

Let There be Light 105

The End from the Beginning 123

Those Who Glow 141

Stepping into the Glory 159

About the Author 171

FOREWORD

My husband and I met Dr. Bruce Allen in Singapore in a prophetic conference where Prophet Sadhu Sundar Selvaraj was also ministering.

Since then we have also met his lovely wife, Reshma, and had the privilege to fellowship with both of them on many occasions.

They are faithful ministers of the Gospel of the Kingdom.

Dr. Bruce's ministry brings the revelatory light of the truth from the Scriptures, releasing the manifestation of that revelation from the spiritual realm into the natural realm.

With simplicity, he captivates his audience's attention, encouraging, training, and leading them to experience and walk in the supernatural.

Bruce has been instrumental for transformation in the lives of many believers.

As a speaker in conferences around the world, as a teacher in his schools of the supernatural, and as an author, he has released many people to move in the power and liberty of the Holy Spirit into realms they had never imagined possible.

Such is the power the Lord always intended His people to operate in, especially in these last days before the Lord Jesus Christ returns as King.

He reminds me of the words written in the book of Mark

chapter 16 verse 20 where Heaven and the believers work together:

And they went forth, and preached every where, the Lord working with them, and confirming the word with signs following. Amen (KJV).

Foundations of Glory is a book designed and inspired from Heaven to destroy any trace of unbelief that might have entered into the heart of a child of God by revealing the light of his/her true identity.

This book can transform the reader's life just by following the simple steps of faith, shown no longer to be earthbound!

You will be amazed at the results.

I have been greatly blessed, inspired, and instructed by this book and highly recommend it.

Whether pastor or sheep, whosoever is passionate and hungry for more of God in their life, for a deeper understanding of God's glory, and for true readiness to meet the soon-coming King Jesus, this is the book for you.

Pastor Stella Roco
Mahanaim Life Ministry

1

REVELATION, AN OPEN DOOR

For the last 17 years on Rosh Hashanah, I have had a visitation from the Lord that has impacted my life greatly. For those of you who are unfamiliar with what Rosh Hashanah is, let me explain.

Rosh Hashanah literally means the "beginning or head" of the year and is the Jewish New Year. The biblical name for this holiday is Yom Teruah, literally "day of shouting/ blasting." It is the first of the Jewish High Holy Days, Yamim Nora'im, or "Days of Awe" specified by Leviticus 23:23-32, which usually occur in the early autumn months of September or October.

Rosh Hashanah is a two-day celebration that begins on the first day of Tishrei. Tishrei is the first month of the Jewish civil year, but the seventh month of the ecclesiastical year.

At these times of visitation on Rosh Hashanah I was told I was to record what I was being shown and understand what the Lord was prophetically communicating because it was a message to the church. I want to emphatically state that these experiences were nothing that I ever asked for and they are not about me personally, although as part of the church I too am to receive these prophetic messages and take them to heart.

Rosh Hashanah, October 3-4, 2016 was one of the most unusual encounters I've had to date. I didn't know quite how to share this until a couple of months after the experience, and by then the Lord had been giving me greater clarity and understanding of what I had witnessed and experienced.

Many times, when I have been visited by the Lord, He has communicated to me through visions. Most believers do not understand that visions are language. If we understand that one third of the Bible came through dreams and visions and that God communicates through dreams and visions, we realize we are "hearing His voice." It was never meant to be an unusual occurrence for a select few.

One third of the bible came through dreams and visions

Many years ago, the Lord said to me in a visitation, "My sheep know My voice, so you should expect visions and dreams. That is the voice of God."

Like myself, and millions of others, you can and will experience visions in many different and personally significant ways.

In many of my personal experiences, the Lord has come as my Best Friend. I love ministering this concept to the youth and seeing how they just embrace that close, non-religious relationship with the Lord. We talk about just "kicking it" or "hanging out" with Jesus, and that resonates with them.

They hate religion, but they love relationship. Jesus has been my best friend for a long time.

Jesus has manifested himself to me as:

- Healer and Comforter
- Bridegroom and Lover of My Soul
- King of Glory
- My Best Friend
- My High Priest

I have encountered Him in so many ways with different facets of His character being exemplified that I cannot enumerate them all. This last Rosh Hashanah, which began at sundown on October 2, 2016, He came to me as the King of Glory.

The Visitation of the Lord

Throughout the past 17 years each time I've had an encounter with the Lord during this festive season of Rosh Hashanah it was during a time of focused worship. For me, that is the attitude that seems to attune my senses and my heart upon the Lord and the spiritual dimension.

This time was no different. I chose to come before the Lord with intent, expectation, and worship while in a service in Manila. Over time it has become second nature for me to close out the activities of the surrounding crowds of those worshiping in a service or even when I am alone at home.

While standing in that service with 10,000 other voices

raised to Him in worship and adoration, I heard the still small voice of the Lord. He said, "Come up here."

Let me tell you, when the Lord says that to you, it is beyond explanation or our ability to communicate! The only way that I can describe this is that every cell, every atom of your body just explodes in joy, just overwhelming joy, and suddenly you are there with Him!

Immediately I found myself standing before Jesus in the heavenly realm. Behind Him I saw what looked like a massive building that put me in remembrance of Solomon's Temple described in Scripture.

The temple of God is the very Throne of God. Just as we are the temple of the Holy Spirit, so the very presence of the Lord is the temple if you can understand that. Before this place of His majesty was the sea of glass.

As I was looking at Jesus it was as if we were standing upon a slight rise so the scene behind Him was what looked like a valley from our perspective. I cannot categorically say this was in fact the case, but it seemed that way to me at the time.

As I looked over Jesus' shoulder there were, it seemed, billions of people on the Sea of Glass before the throne, standing silently with a palpable sense of expectation, as if they were awaiting a proclamation.

My attention was wholly upon Jesus, yet at the same time I could see and take in everything around us at once. I cannot explain this totality of awareness that is granted when in that dimension other than to say I was "plugged in" to the whole of this vast place.

Upon His head was a crown of glory—a multi-faceted, multi-jeweled crown that was both reflecting His glory in bright living colors and resonating with life, light, and worship.

He was wearing a purple robe of a living material unlike anything I've ever seen before. His bearing was regal and captivating all at once. There was an unmistakable dignity, authority, power, and majesty resonating out from within Him. In a word, He was the King.

The most amazing thing was seeing light come from the wounds in His hands, feet, and side! From those wounds, in that light, we found life!

> In the presence of God the flesh is quiet

This experience was something other than a casual encounter where someone says, "I want to show you something." This was a declaration by a monarch, a king, the King of Glory, and He came to proclaim something.

In situations like this, your flesh is not in the predominant position, trust me. Your flesh has a voice and it speaks very loudly all the time down here, but when you get there, in the presence of God, the flesh is quiet.

The only thing I could do, the only thing anyone would be able to do when you come into His presence like that is to worship. So immediately, I fell on my face. I had no choice and no recourse.

There was something in my spirit in this holy moment that said, "Lord, everything You have ever blessed me with in my life, every revelation, every experience, all of my life, I just lay it at Your feet." I recognized with a supernatural clarity the futility and frailty of human flesh and human endeavor and my overwhelming need of Him.

I love the story of Abram who left Ur of the Chaldees because he heard the voice of the Lord (see Gen. 12:1). He did not hesitate; he immediately obeyed what he heard (see Gen. 12:4). I recalled when Abram was given a promise of an heir, his son Isaac (see Gen. 18:10).

This man's faith would have been unusual faith because there was no voice of God in his day. Yet he heard the voice of God and he followed Him. Abram followed this voice, and God gave him a prophetic promise. He said, "I am going to make your children as the sand of the seas and the stars of Heaven" (see Gen. 22:17).

Keeping the Promise of God Before You

God can sneak up on you, and sometimes you don't even realize it. Abraham was walking around in the desert and all he was seeing every day was sand! At night, all he saw were stars! The biblical principal from this is to keep the promise of God in front of your face, because what you focus on, you will connect with.

Sometimes we take prophetic words and we put them on the shelf of our spiritual display case and we say, "Look at all of these wonderful words I got. How many do you have?" We do not understand foundational biblical principles; therefore, is it any wonder we do not receive biblical answers? Just as Abram did, we are to keep the promises of God before our eyes continually! That is the biblical principle that will release to you the promises of Scripture!

Thirty-three years after Isaac was born, God said, "I want you to go offer him up as a burnt sacrifice" (see Gen. 22:2).

Abraham didn't argue with the Lord. He said, "OK, Isaac, let's go."

So Abraham rose early in the morning and saddled his donkey, and took two of his young men with him, and Isaac his son; and he split the wood for the burnt offering, and arose and went to the place of which God had told him. Then on the third day Abraham lifted his eyes and saw the place afar off. And Abraham said to his young men, "Stay here with the donkey; the lad and I will go yonder and worship, and we will come back to you."

So Abraham took the wood of the burnt offering and laid it on Isaac his son; and he took the fire in his hand, and a knife, and the two of them went together. But Isaac spoke to Abraham his father and said, "My father!"

And he said, "Here I am, my son."

Then he said, "Look, the fire and the wood, but where is the lamb for a burnt offering?"

And Abraham said, "My son, God will provide for Himself the lamb for a burnt offering." So the two of them went together.

Then they came to the place of which God had told him. And Abraham built an altar there and placed the wood in order; and he bound Isaac his son and laid him on the altar, upon the wood. And Abraham stretched out his hand and took the knife to slay his son.

But the Angel of the Lord called to him from heaven and said, "Abraham, Abraham!"

So he said, "Here I am."

> And He said, "Do not lay your hand on the lad, or do anything to him; for now I know that you fear God, since you have not withheld your son, your only son, from Me" (Genesis 22:3-12).

And so that day, the third day, he built an altar, he tied Isaac up, and he placed him on the altar. This was the test he faced: Do you love the God of the promise more than the promise of God?

Isaac was the fulfillment of Abraham's promise and God tested him. Do you love Me more than the promise for your life and for your generations after you? He proved his worthiness because he loved God more.

That was the experience that I had at His feet. That question was resonating in me. Do you love Him more than you love every promise and every good thing that He has ever given you or is going to give to you? That question was a no-brainer for me!

Here is another significant thing about Abraham's experience we need to recognize—this is the first place we see Jehovah Jireh, the "Provider" in Scripture!

> *Then Abraham lifted his eyes and looked, and there behind him was a ram caught in a thicket by its horns. So Abraham went and took the ram, and offered it up for a burnt offering instead of his son. And Abraham called the name of the place, The-Lord-Will-Provide; as it is said to this day, "In the Mount of the Lord it shall be provided" (Genesis 22:13-14).*

Provision comes from a surrendered life and not from the misconception that many have which says, "I gave this for God, so He has to give me something back." There is a vast difference between provision and manipulation!

This was the place that I found myself in that moment, and as realization flooded my being He said to me, "Stand."

Suddenly I was looking at these multitudes, billions of people before the Throne of God. I cannot adequately describe this experience. There was a holy hush. The atmosphere was literally pregnant with anticipation and fulfillment at the same time. I knew there was about to come forth a proclamation from the Father that was strategic in the prophetic stream of time in which we live.

Communication in Heaven is not verbal. Yes, you can communicate that way, but verbal communication is the lower form of communication and as such is limiting and somewhat ineffective. You know how it goes: "I said left,"

"No, you said right." "I said yes," "No, you said no." Those who are married really understand this!

In Heaven, communication is very different. The best descriptor for this found in Scripture is a word of knowledge or an impartation.

Here is another great example for clarity's sake. My wife Reshma is Indo-Fijian—she is East Indian but was born and raised in Fiji. I can tell you about the beautiful sandy beaches in Fiji, the eighty-six degree temperature of the surf, and the water that is so crystal clear. I could go on and on with the description, and I can paint a little bit of a word picture, but I am not really good at that.

However, in the realm of the spirit if I wanted to communicate the beauty of the beach in Fiji it would be complete and overwhelming! You would experience every minute detail of it and there would be no miscommunication whatsoever. You would literally experience it for yourself! That is communication in Heaven.

Therefore, because of this supernatural "knowing" imparted to me, I knew that there was about to come forth a proclamation that had eternal ramifications, and it was significant to the Church on the earth.

Chariots of Fire and the Elijah Generation

Above the Temple/Throne, I saw millions, even hundreds of millions of chariots of fire begin to come forth. This is significant because Jude 14 talks about Enoch being the seventh generation from Adam. Why is this significant? I discuss this in greater detail in my book Prophetic Promise of the 7th Day, but let me give you a short explanation.

In 2 Peter 3:8 it states, "But, beloved, do not forget this one thing, that with the Lord one day is as a thousand years, and a thousand years as one day."

From the days that Jesus walked the earth until the turn of the 21st century we have completed approximately 2,000 years. In line with 2 Peter 3:8, that would prophetically signify two days. We are now early in the morning of the third day.

Historically, we can trace back from Jesus 4,000 years to the time of Adam. From Adam until the turn of the century we have completed 6,000 years, or six days. Therefore, we are also early in the morning of the seventh day. We are an Enoch generation—the seventh from Adam! We will have the privilege of walking with God, and we will "be not" because we will be caught up to ever be with the Lord just as Enoch was!

We are also an Elijah generation. Doesn't Scripture say that before the return of Jesus there is going to come forth a people walking in the spirit and the power of Elijah?

> *Behold, I will send you Elijah the prophet before the coming of the great and dreadful day of the Lord (Malachi 4:5).*

That is this generation! In 2 Kings 2:11 Elijah went home in a chariot of fire! It is very significant what God was communicating to me in this visitation.

As I listened in Heaven, the proclamation that came forth was that we are moving into the final dispensation where God is going to see every prophetic promise in Scripture fulfilled and every destiny that He has begun within the lives of His people completed. This is because "He who calls you is faithful, who also will do it" (1 Thess. 5:24). We have transitioned into a day, a season, of completion!

Enoch and the Book of Mysteries

At this time, I found myself once again able to stand, and so I arose and stood facing Jesus.

I was completely in awe of this whole experience, marveling at the sensory overload and the tangible effusive love of God that was the very atmosphere around me. As I was basking in this love, I noticed an individual separate himself from the multitudes. He began to walk toward us up this slight incline, and I noticed he was carrying a huge book similar to those old family Bibles you see sometimes on people's coffee tables.

Again, beyond the veil you know even as also you are known. I immediately recognized (by the spirit) that this individual was Enoch.

I became very excited and a bit overwhelmed because I have always wanted to meet Enoch, thinking that one day when we are all together in Heaven my opportunity would come. Now, here he was! Immediately I noticed he was not a very tall individual, yet his presence was overwhelming.

The spirit of revelation and holiness effusively emanated from him accompanied with a sweet fragrance.

I remember thinking, "I love encountering and experiencing the things of Heaven!"

As he was approaching, I could see he was holding the book with both hands, pressing it close to his chest as if it were something precious. This piqued my interest and I became very curious about what this volume was that was so precious to him. I kept thinking, "What is this book that Enoch is holding?"

As he came alongside Jesus, without saying a word he extended the book toward me. I was a little bit surprised, and as I grasped the book I asked him, "Sir, what is this?" He said, "This is the Book of Mysteries that the Lord gave me when I walked on this earth."

Then he continued, "Now take and finish it."

I began to tremble with the power and glory that was released through his words and the object that I was now holding in my hands. Great fear came upon me and I became very weak. I was absolutely speechless with awe.

He then handed me his mantle and indicated I was to put it on. How can I describe this experience? Words fail. To say I was overcome is not sufficient. Joy, fear, awe, ecstasy, love, unworthiness, and any other word used cannot express the immediate rush of emotion and reverence that flowed through my consciousness. I was literally undone!

In awe and excitement, I asked him, "Would you lay your hands on me and bless me?"

He responded with amusement in his voice, "No."

He said, "The Lord has already blessed and commissioned you!"

Then I turned to the Lord, and He spoke. And this is what He said:

"Go and do all I have commanded of you. I have given you insight, and you have received My purposes and desire for your life. Now I will give you understanding. As you have met Enoch this night and have received his book of mysteries, so, too, you shall receive of his mantle that has been prepared for this day. Move forward in faith and do not hold back. Now the hour is come for My glory to be revealed in you. Trust Me to perform all that I said I would do, for it shall surely come to pass now."

2

THE DESTINY OF GOD

We are in a season of profound fulfillment of the promises of God for our lives and our generation. I know that someone just read the previous chapter and you are saying in your heart, "Well, I don't know exactly what I am supposed to do." Please understand this. The Lord has already deposited your destiny in your heart.

So many people have come to me and said, "You know, I don't know what I am called to do in ministry."

> We are in a season of profound fulfillment of the promises of God

It is really not hard. Scripture says, "Whatever your hand finds to do, do it with all your might" (Eccles. 9:10)—that's the first thing. Second, what is in your heart?

Someone might say, "I love working with children!" Well, get busy! Someone else might say, "I like to teach." Then start preparing! Position yourself. Do you understand? If there is a desire in your heart, pay attention to that because the Scripture says the Lord will give you the desires of your heart (see Ps. 37:4). What we have not realized is that desire for service—whatever form it may be—comes from God! He gave you the desire that is in your heart!

We have misconstrued that for years, for generations even. We have treated this promise as if Jesus is a genie in a bottle and if we want something He is required to give it to us.

Allow me to give you a more accurate interpretation of Psalms 37:4: "The Lord will birth within you a desire according to the destiny He has placed within you, and because He birthed that desire, He will fulfill it."

Do you see it now? The Lord places a desire in your heart! And because He put that desire in your heart, He is leading you to the fulfillment of that dream and vision. He will give you the desire of your heart. Faithful is He who called, who also shall do it (see 1 Thess. 5:24)!

I have heard time and time again believers express their longing and desire for the Lord as if they were the ones who made a decision one day to be hungry for more of Him. No, God is the one who put that hunger in you. That is the grace of God. Count yourself blessed that you have a passion for Jesus, and pray for those who don't, because He has called you to be a forerunner in this.

Over the years I've met so many people who feel their decision for Christ was made entirely on their own and their desire to live for Christ is theirs, too. I don't know all the reasons why we are like this in western culture, but please allow me to share a little bit of the light that I do have on this subject.

In short, we have a Greco-Roman mindset. We feel that we have to figure it all out, we have to quantify, and as we do so we check off our "religious to do list" to step into our destiny. We have been programed to believe that there must be a certain number of "steps" to take in order to attain to a certain standard or level of spirituality.

Do you know what? Jesus just had one. In John 5:19, He says, "Then Jesus answered and said to them, 'Most assuredly, I say to you, the Son can do nothing of Himself, but what He sees the Father do; for whatever He does, the Son also does in like manner.'"

Jesus asserts His dependence on the Father and His distinct role subordinate to the Father's will and plan.

I love the way Jesus conducted His life and ministry! I am going to share how some of this unfolded and became life-changing for me because it is important for us to get past religious thinking and get to the reality of the Word. Some of us have been going around the same mountain for years, and we continue being frustrated because we don't really understand why our attempts to accomplish His will for our lives doesn't seem to work. The reality is that every one of us has faced this same issue at some time.

About 19 years ago, I was ministering in Oklahoma City, Oklahoma, and the Lord spoke to me. It has become my habit to always pray in the New Year (according to our western calendar) as well as the Hebrew New Year, Rosh Hashanah, allowing the Lord to share His will and His heart with me for the year.

In this particular year, the Lord said to me, "I want you to study one word from the Scriptures this year."

I said, "OK. What word?"

He responded, "I want you to study the word name."

I said to myself, "Well, that is just weird enough to be God. One word, the word 'name.' I should be able to do this pretty quickly."

So, I began to study the word 'name'. The further I got, the more fascinated I became until a whole year had passed and I had still not completed my study! I didn't share about what the Lord was unveiling to me for almost ten years. I just let that revelation work in me. Keep in mind that just because God gives you something, that doesn't mean you are supposed to immediately share it.

As Many as Received Him

This is something that I learned many years ago. I don't study Scripture so that I might have a message to share; rather, I study Scripture because that is my Love Letter from my God. I study the Word to know Him, and the overflow of that relationship is what I get to share. The difference? One message is like delivering a book report and the other is sharing living revelation based on the intimate knowledge of the person of God. Of course, some of us may find it much easier to share a message that is based upon our own ability to study and gather information.

So, it was just two years ago that the Lord spoke to me once again about this study and the revelation I had received, and He said, "Share it." I'm excited about this because I believe that what I am going to share with you will radically change your life and your understanding of who you are called to be!

> *But as many as received him, to them gave he power to become the sons of God, even to them that believe on his name (John 1:12 KJV).*

In John 1:12 it says "as many as received Him." Now, stop and think about this for a minute. "As many as received Him." This is a classic salvation Scripture. Have you received Jesus yet? The Word says, as many as received Him—that speaks of salvation.

Now look what it says next. "To them He gave the right [or the power, or the privilege] to become sons of God." Do you notice it doesn't say as many as received Him were sons of God?

In the New American Standard Bible, it says it this way: "But as many as received Him, to them He gave the right to become children of God, even to those who believe in His name."

Sons of God

This is the doctrine that most of the Church teaches—if you are born again, you are a son of God. That is not what Scripture says. There is a process from birth to becoming a son, if you understand Hebrew culture.

You see, we have always colored this scripture with a western mindset. In our western culture, we can have a baby and say, "Do you see my one-day-old baby boy? That's my son." But in Hebrew culture they say, "That is my child."

> *For unto us a child is born, unto us a son is given: and the government shall be upon his shoulder: and his name shall be called Wonderful, Counsellor, The mighty God, The everlasting Father, The Prince of Peace (Isaiah 9:6 KJV).*

There is a gap of many years difference between a child being born and a son given, and it has to do with a process of maturity in Hebrew culture. That is why when you accept Christ, you are born again and now you have the privilege, the right, or the power to become a son if you submit yourself to the process.

We understand the Scripture or we have heard the Scripture that states we are to work out our own salvation. That speaks of a process, not an instant transformation.

> *Wherefore, my beloved, as ye have always obeyed, not as in my presence only, but now much more in my absence, work out your own salvation with fear and trembling (Philippians 2:12 KJV).*

Therefore, it is a misnomer in the Church when they say, "We save souls." No, we don't save souls. The saving of a soul is a life-long process of being conformed to Christ. We see people redeemed out of darkness into light, so we see their spirit reborn, but we don't really save souls. In the book of Proverbs (11:30) is a better rendering of a verse with which most of us are familiar.

> *The fruit of the righteous is a tree of life; and he that winneth souls is wise (Proverbs 11:30 KJV).*

Moving back to the Hebrew language and a Hebrew

cultural understanding will help you to discover the concept of the process of salvation. Working out your salvation is a process of the transformation of our souls. We move away from the tree of the knowledge of good and evil and toward the conforming of ourselves by faith to the Tree of Life that is in our spirit. We transition from intellect to spirit. I am not against intellect in any way if it is sanctified, but there is a big difference.

We transition from intellect to spirit

Sanctified Imagination

The imagination also needs to be sanctified, as does the soul, but most people never even consider dealing with their intellect or their imagination; they just let it wander in an undisciplined manner. However, Scripture says in 2 Corinthians 10:5 we are to "[Cast] down imaginations, and every high thing that exalteth itself against the knowledge of God, and bringing into captivity every thought to the obedience of Christ" (KJV).

So, we discover there is a discipline that is necessary in every believer's life. This is where the rubber meets the road in the process of working out our salvation. Many don't like discipline, but can I tell you something? You are never going to grow up and become a mature son or daughter if you don't submit yourself to this process.

Why is this important? Everywhere we go people say, "I want the easy five-step, three-step, whatever program." The truth is that there is no easy five-step program.

As you go through this process, there will be difficult times, but the thing that will carry you through during the difficult times is passion for Him. Submission to a process and passion for Jesus will get you through. That is the key to our advancement in the Kingdom in a nutshell.

3

COVENANTS

I have to present to you an understanding of covenants. It is intrinsic to the process we are discussing and will give you greater understanding, not only of this process but of your growing intimacy with the Lord.

In Hebrew culture, there are four major covenants we find in Scripture. There are other lesser covenants also, but the four major covenants are the most telling, and they are very important. If you understand them, your life and your understanding of Scripture will be transformed.

Every covenant is initiated by God, and every covenant must have a respondent—someone who will enter into that covenant with the Lord. The very first covenant we see was in the Garden of Eden when Adam and Eve sinned. They broke covenant with God. Now, think about this for a moment—according to Scripture, a day is as a thousand years:

> *But, beloved, be not ignorant of this one thing, that one day is with the Lord as a thousand years, and a thousand years as one day (2 Peter 3:8 KJV).*

If a day is as a thousand years and man was created on the sixth day, you will notice that it doesn't say what part of the sixth day the event occurred. The question then is, at what point on this thousand-year "day" was Adam created? And at what point was Eve brought forth?

We have the sixth day on which Adam and Eve were created, and then there was a seventh day, a day of rest. That would indicate that somewhere after the seventh day of rest came the temptation, and sin was entered into. Adam and Eve walked and talked face to face with God every day, and for all that, they were still susceptible to deception and they rejected or chose to "divorce" the Lord.

This was not an immediate conversion or falling away process. It took time for the seeds of deception the serpent was sowing to take root and to grow. When they did, the outcome was separation from intimacy with the Lord.

The devil will try to do this also in your life. If you pay attention you can see the way he plants a seed. And after a while you start "gnawing" or meditating upon that seed. You begin to think about it, to meditate upon it, and eventually it drops into your heart and becomes your reality. You then speak it forth and it produces. It releases that "living" death in you.

This was the process that went on until finally Eve, by constantly meditating on the "benefits" of eating of that tree, gave in. She ate of the fruit and Adam ate of the fruit with her.

An interesting insight on this is that Adam, being the first Adam, was not deceived but chose to suffer the consequences of a fall from grace because of his love for Eve. He willingly chose to suffer with her. In the same way, Jesus, the Second

Adam, chose to come to this earth to be tempted and suffer on our behalf to see us freed from this curse.

So, they gave God a writing of divorce. In effect, Adam and Eve said to God, "We choose to follow the serpent rather than You. We choose allegiance to his promises rather than to Your promises."

Our Covering

Of course, it broke the Father's heart, but His response then is the same as it is today—He gives us a way of escape and redemption. Immediately the Father slew an animal and put a covering on them. He made an atonement by the blood sacrifice of an animal and that covering was symbolic of the Lamb that was slain from the foundation of the world—Jesus.

There is an interesting correlation between the covering God put upon Adam and Eve and the bridal garment used in a Hebrew marriage ceremony.

In Hebrew culture, there are four layers of fine linen that go into the making of a bridal garment. The bridegroom only has one layer. Every guest that comes in to a wedding has to have a white linen garment on. It honors the bride and groom and speaks of purity in their union.

> *But when the king came in to look at the guests, he saw there a man who had no wedding garment. And he said to him, "Friend, how did you get in here without a wedding garment?" And he was speechless (Matthew 22:11-12 ESV).*

Going back to the Genesis account (Gen. 3:20), let me explain what the Lord covered them with. In Hebrew culture a bridal garment has four layers of fine linen. The first layer, or the undergarment of a bridal garment, was called the ketonet.

In the Hebrew text, the word for the garment the Lord gave to cover Adam and Eve was ketonet. By doing so, the Lord immediately initiated a process and extended an invitation whereby mankind may come back into bridal intimacy with the Father. This was the first covenant, ratified in blood. We would know this as the blood covenant.

The Blood

Those who receive Jesus as Lord and Savior enter into the blood covenant established by the sacrifice of Jesus' blood on the cross. Another name for this covenant is servant covenant. Now, here's something about the initial blood covenant that most westerners don't understand. The blood covenant must be renewed every day! It is not a once-only application of the blood that is sufficient.

We do know that Jesus became the sacrifice once and for all and there is no longer a need to offer the blood of a sacrificial animal to cover our sins. However, the principle is the same. We are to be continuously washed in the blood.

That means we are to be quick to repent, slow to speak, slow to anger. Quick to repent. Stay clean. Keep your garment clean before Him. "Father, forgive me; I don't want to grieve You. I repent."

There is a gospel of "greasy grace" that is being preached in this hour. It is not new! Throughout church history there have been those who used the gift of God's grace as a license to sin. The embracing of this false gospel leads to apostasy.

Its basic tenet is once you are born again and cleansed by the blood of Jesus, you are free to live your life in any manner you see fit. You can commit any form of unrighteousness, participate in any perverse lifestyle you choose, partake of any substance, and abuse your body, treat others with contempt and disdain, and not worry because you are "saved" and it's OK. Jesus forgave you once, and you are forever forgiven of anything you now do.

No! I tell you emphatically, no! Out of the same pulpits of those teaching this false doctrine comes the instruction that we don't even need to read the gospels anymore because that was before the cross and it is irrelevant. And many teach that we should not say the Lord's Prayer as Jesus taught His disciples to pray, because we don't say "forgive us our sins" as we are already forgiven. And by the way, some say, "Paul didn't really have a revelation of grace." That is how crazy that message of "grace" has become, and the masses love it because it caters to the sinful flesh. It is a doctrine of demons.

> Grace is not a license to sin, but it is the power of God to keep us from sin!

All of these examples come via firsthand exposure to those teaching this heresy. Grace is not a license to sin, but it is the power of God to keep us from sin! It is and always will be a tutor that leads us to righteousness!

Again, the blood covenant must be renewed every day. We renew it by confessing our sin and allowing the blood of Jesus to once again cleanse us. If I'm angry without cause—that is sin. If I tell a "little white lie," an untruth—that is sin. If I covet, lust, have evil intent—that is sin. A confession and repentance is a renewal of the blood covenant.

Jesus says that He doesn't want any to perish but all to come to a saving knowledge of God. Keep yourself and your life cleansed by the blood of the Lamb!

> *This is good, and it is pleasing in the sight of God our Savior, who desires all people to be saved and to come to the knowledge of the truth (1 Timothy 2:3-4 ESV).*

The Salt Covenant

We see that the first covenant was initiated by the Lord and it is available to anybody, but there has got to be somebody to respond. The unfortunate truth is that not all will respond. Remember, it is not the Lord's will that any should perish, but that all should be saved (see 2 Pet. 3:9). Yet we know that not everyone avails themselves of this free gift.

Likewise at some point in your Christian walk, the Lord initiates a second level of covenant and it is called the salt covenant. In ancient times, salt was a precious commodity, so it spoke of wealth and would often be used as a form of currency to trade. They would weigh and measure out a certain portion in exchange for goods and services. It was not uncommon to see men carrying a pouch of salt on their belt.

Another name for the salt covenant is the friendship covenant. You choose to commit to a level of intimacy agreed to by two people who love and respect one another. This is how the salt covenant is enacted: If two people, say you and I, wanted to enter into this level of covenant, we would agree to meet together at a certain time and on a certain day. At that time, we would place a small bowl between us. You would take some salt from your pouch and I would take some salt from mine. We would then place a pinch of our salt into the bowl and mix it.

After a statement of commitment or a prayer, we would each take some bread, dip it into the salt, and eat it. At this point we have broken bread and shared a meal together and we have entered into this covenant of friendship.

This covenant is considered eternal and can never be broken or rescinded. Unlike the blood covenant, this covenant does not have to be renewed every day.

Let me give you some insight into the Scriptures that few in the western world understand. Our Bible is made up of two major sections that we call the Old Testament and the New Testament. In Hebrew it would be called the Old Covenant and the B'rit Hadashah, which is Hebrew for "Renewed Covenant" or "New Testament" as we've come to know it. Or you could also say that we have the Old Covenant and the Renewed Covenant.

In Hebraic understanding, each covenant builds upon the previous covenant. We do not have one covenant replacing or doing away with another. So the blood covenant that was the first covenant established is concurrently in effect with this second covenant, the salt covenant. And so it goes through all four covenants. Each covenant does not do away with the previous covenant(s) but is a continuation and building toward something greater.

In Hebraic understanding, each covenant builds upon the previous covenant.

And so it goes through all four covenants. Each covenant does not do away with the previous covenant(s) but is a continuation and building toward something greater.

Similarly, the "New Testament" does not do away with the "Old Testament." The ordinances and laws were done away with but only because the Renewed Covenant (New Testament) shows with greater clarity what the old was pointing to all along—a redeemer would come who would give us the ability, through His sacrifice, to keep the law and the prophets because it is now written in our hearts.

With this understanding in mind, we realize that just because an individual has entered into this next level of covenant, that of friendship, it does not indicate that they are no longer a servant. Just as Jesus was the greatest of all because He was a servant of all, that does not take away from the fact He was the Son of God. He was both.

The Sandal Covenant

It is imperative we understand these things because this is basic Bible, albeit from a Hebrew perspective. At some point, there is another level of covenant that we enter into in our walk, and the Lord initiates this one also. It is called the sandal covenant.

The sandal covenant has nothing to do with sandals per se, except that the Hebrews were instructed to take their old sandals and mark out the borders of their inheritance. This tradition of using sandals then became synonymous with an individual's inheritance. The first-born son would receive his inheritance when he came of age. Therefore, it was called the sandal covenant. This speaks of sonship and inheritance.

Interestingly, when Moses came to the burning bush, the Lord told him, "Take your sandals off your feet, for the place where you stand is holy ground" (Exod. 3:5).

There are many different facets of revelation to be gleaned from this particular scripture, but what I want you to focus on is the fact he was told to take his sandals off. Or in other words, "Moses, get ready to mark out your inheritance."

Moses did not come to the place of inheritance until he was 80 years old! Why, you may ask? In each individual life only our Father knows when we are ready to enter in to the promise, destiny, or inheritance allotted to us as our portion.

You don't get to your inheritance until you go through a season of brokenness. You don't get to your promise until the Lord deems your character is sufficient enough for you not be in grave danger of being destroyed by the task before you. Study the life of not only Moses, but all of the patriarchs and you will see a clear picture of this principle.

In the Hebrew culture there came a day in the life of the first-born son when the father would deem that his son has matured to the point of a pre-determined acceptability—a standard set by that father, whereby he was now ready to be recognized as a son and joint heir.

At this time, the father would take that son before the gates of the city, the place where the leaders of the city sat and dispensed business and commerce was transacted, and pronounce at the top of his voice, "Today I adopt you as my son and joint heir!"

All the elders seated at the gates would be a witness to the fact that this young man was now a mature son and able to be entrusted with matters pertaining to the family and whatever business they may have.

Remember the scripture: "Unto us a Child is born, unto us a son is given" (Isa. 9:6).

Jesus went into the Jordan River and was baptized of John, and when he came out of the water, what is it that happened? The Father spoke: "This is My beloved Son!"

And lo a voice from heaven, saying, This is my beloved Son, in whom I am well pleased (Matthew 3:17 KJV).

Jesus received His public announcement of sonship at 30 years of age! Until that point, He had submitted Himself to tutors. He submitted Himself to a process of sanctification, of separation for three and a half years of ministry. Thirty years of preparation and the development of His character for three and a half years of ministry. Think about that!

The Bridal Covenant

Now, at some point in this journey in Christ, at a time chosen by the Father, we enter into the fourth covenant, which is the bridal covenant.

In 2015 on Rosh Hashanah, Jesus appeared to me in a meeting we were participating in. The Lord was standing in front of me wearing a red robe, sandals, and a white garment underneath, and He was holding a little, nondescript box.

I said, "Lord, what is that?"

I like presents and surprises as much as anyone.

He smiled and said, "Well, come here and look."

So I went over and He opened the box, and inside the box was a ring. I said, "Oh! That's beautiful!"

He said, "No. Look closer!"

In the spirit realm, space and time does not work like it does here in our physical world. As I looked at this ring, it transformed! There was kind of a "whoosh!" sound and instantly the ring was enlarged! It was a beautiful setting and the stone looked like a diamond, but I knew it wasn't a diamond. The ring, the stone, was alive, and it was worshiping the Lord!

Have you ever seen a drop of food coloring dropped into water? As it hits the water it expands in unusual shapes and sizes with the colors shifting with the light in the glass. That's how the interior of this beautiful diamond-looking stone appeared. The substance "floating" and moving in the stone was a vibrant red.

He said, "I am now proposing to My Bride."

I asked the Lord, "What is that?"

He said, "That's My blood. That is what you hear speaking and worshiping. It is the bridal price."

He said, "I am now proposing to My Bride."

This happened two years ago. Meditate on that.

When the bride agrees to the contract of marriage, at the betrothal is when you are married. That takes place before the consummation of the marriage. My wife, Reshma, and I had a betrothal ceremony according to her culture a year before we got married. I actually felt like I was married, and I finally understood and got a revelation of biblical betrothal. Some might say that it was an engagement. No, it was beyond engagement because we actually went through a ceremony where we exchanged rings and vows. It was a betrothal. It was a contract, a covenant.

The average time between betrothal and when the

bridegroom comes for his bride to take her to the place he has prepared is between one to one and a half years!

Another thought to ponder. In our world as men we understand the idea of "Don't you dare touch my bride!" We will stand up and fight for her and protect her even at the cost of our own lives.

In the same way I believe Jesus will not tolerate anyone who has the intention of harming His Bride! He will fight for her and protect her! The Bride also takes on His name or His character.

We enter in through the blood covenant or the servant covenant, which we maintain every day (renew) through repentance and confession. We remain a servant forever, even though we become a friend, a son, or the bride.

We then enter into friendship via the salt covenant. Again, because these covenants build upon one another, we are still servants, only now we enter into a deeper level of intimacy—that of friendship.

In the same way, the sandal covenant or sonship covenant reflects a deepening level of intimacy and relationship. And the final covenant or bridal covenant speaks of the greatest level of intimacy we can have. You see, the whole process is about relationship. It is graphically described in Scripture in the Hebrew covenants, and it is very, very obvious when you see it.

To as many as received Him, to them He gave the right to become the son (daughter) of God.

4

THE CHARACTER OF CHRIST

Many people embrace a nominal Christian experience or a religious experience and think that is the whole of Christianity. That is a fallacy. Salvation is the starting point.

That's why I am grateful for the revelation of the four covenants that we covered in our previous chapter, because they reveal that we are in a process of growing up to be like Him.

What's in a Name?

Once again, let's get back to the study of the word name.

In the year 2000, during the New Year's festivities, as I was waiting upon the Lord I inquired of Him what He was saying for the next year, 2001.

As clearly as I've ever heard Him, He said, "I want you to study one word this year."

I was intrigued, and so asked Him, "What word, Lord?"

He said, "The word name."

That began an adventure that continues to this day and has drastically changed my understanding of Scripture and challenged me in an ever-increasing way.

I got out my old Strong's Concordance and began my search.

I discovered in the Old Covenant the word name, in every instance but two, means character, honor, and authority. In the Renewed Covenant, the word name means, in every instance but one, character and authority.

> *The name of the Lord is a strong [fortified] tower; the righteous run to it and are safe (Proverbs 18:10).*

If you are like me you may have always wondered, "What does that mean?" How can His "name" be a strong or fortified tower? Well, let me explain that to you.

As I understand what the meaning of the Hebrew word for name means, then I begin to glean a better insight into what is being communicated here. Remember, in the Old Testament, that word name means "character, honor, authority." So we could actually read Proverbs 18:10 this way: "The character of the Lord is a strong tower. The righteous are conformed to it and are safe."

Does that make sense? Does it help you to understand in a more meaningful way what was intended here? The word name speaks of the character of the Lord. Where the Lord's character is evidenced there will also be a greater demonstration of His power, and it will bring honor to the one intended—the Lord!

All throughout Scripture we see the importance of character. In Romans 8:29 does it say that Jesus is the firstborn among "just a handful" of brethren? No! He is the firstborn among many brethren.

> *For whom He foreknew, He also predestined to be conformed to the image of His Son, that He might*

> *be the firstborn among many brethren (Romans 8:29).*

Rather than being the exception, Jesus made a way for all of us to be conformed to the same stature and character that He walked in—that of the Father.

This speaks of the name and the character of the Lord, and it also speaks of His authority. You cannot have the character of God without having the authority of God because they are intrinsically entwined. You can, however, have a measure of authority without character because the gifting and calling of God is without repentance. You can exercise a gift to the extent that you become very proficient, and people will be very impressed by the miraculous manifestations and heap accolades upon you.

The sad fact is, many have become very adept in their gifting, yet their character is repugnant to God. Gifting will take you a certain distance, but it won't carry you home. It does not justify you nor earn you accolades in the courts of Heaven apart from Christ-like character.

> *Many will say to Me in that day, "Lord, Lord, have we not prophesied in Your name, cast out demons in Your name, and done many wonders in Your name?" And then I will declare to them, "I never knew you; depart from Me, you who practice lawlessness!" (Mathew 7:22-23)*

You see, we have taken "in the name of Jesus," and we have made a formula out of a phrase when what Scripture is really trying to communicate to us is a principle for life! I am not against anyone praying "in the name of Jesus." What I want you to see is the deeper meaning and significance of this.

Character! We are speaking of character. We find this truth reiterated time and again throughout Scripture. Let's look at some examples.

In Genesis the Lord is talking to Abram and He reveals a concept often missed in our cultural mindset:

> *No longer shall your name be called Abram, but your name shall be Abraham; for I have made you a father of many nations (Genesis 17:5).*

He says no longer shall your name, or no longer shall your character, be Abram. Why is this important? Because he had a destiny, and the Lord says, "I have got to conform you to My image so that you can fulfill that destiny."

> The Lord had to change Abram's character to such an extent that he could fulfill his destiny!

In order to do that, I have got to change your character. No longer shall your character be Abram, but your character shall be Abraham, for I have made you a father of many nations.

The name Abram means "exalted father," but Abraham means "father of a multitude."

This is why the Church has been so weak and anemic. We have become a bunch of misdirected people with no depth of character, and the world looks at us and sees no reason to come to Christ. They're thinking we are no different than they are, and to a great extent they are right.

However, we are growing up now! We are in a season of insight and revelation being released, which is causing us to understand who and what we truly are! With revelation knowledge comes wisdom and power in order that we can access and walk in that revelation.

> *Then God said to Abraham, "As for Sarai your wife, you shall not call her name Sarai, but Sarah shall be her name. And I will bless her and also give you a son by her; then I will bless her, and she shall be a mother of nations; kings of peoples shall be from her" (Genesis 17:15-16).*

Her name (character) is transitioning from "princess" (Sarai) to "princess of a multitude" (Sarah).

If there had to be a commensurate change of character for Abraham and Sarah to fulfill the prophetic destiny of their lives, perhaps we need to consider that we also may need a change of our character so we can fulfill what God has called us to.

Over the ten years that I meditated and chewed on this revelation, I started reading the gospels to really look at the character of Jesus. That took me on a journey to both the Old and New Covenant because Jesus is talked about in both covenants. His character is expressed and revealed in the Old, and then it is portrayed and demonstrated in the New. It is expressed and portrayed in the New Covenant so it can be expressed and portrayed in our lives.

As I started studying His character, I said, "You know, Lord, I like the way You minister better than what I see in the church."

Let me explain. From the age of 14 when I (as well as the rest of my family) accepted Jesus, I attended a small, independent charismatic church. It all started when my dad got saved in a Full Gospel Businessmen's Fellowship luncheon in Seattle, Washington in October, 1973. His life was so impacted by this group that he became very involved in the organization, even to the point of becoming the President and then an International Director of the Seattle chapter.

So, for the first six years of my Christian life I would attend as many meetings with my dad as I could because I was hungry for the things of God. I was taught that everyone could be involved, even a 14-year-old teenager, and we were encouraged, according to Scripture, to pray for one another (see James 5:16).

This was my introduction to the Christian life—involvement and doing the Word, not just hearing about what others were doing according to the Word.

Then I went to Bible college, and I had a rude awakening! I was told that I was not allowed to pray for my friends or lay hands on the sick because I had no authority to do so!

To say that I was confused is an understatement! This was a major Pentecostal Bible college that purportedly believed in the gifts of and acts of the Holy Spirit!

As far as I knew, the mandate of Scripture was clear:

> *And as you go, preach, saying, "The kingdom of heaven is at hand." Heal the sick, cleanse the lepers, raise the dead, cast out demons. Freely you have received, freely give (Matthew 10:7-8).*
>
> *And He said to them, "Go into all the world and preach the gospel to every creature. He who believes and is baptized will be saved; but he who does not believe will be condemned. And these signs will follow those who believe: In My name they will cast out demons; they will speak with new tongues; they will take up serpents; and if they drink anything deadly, it will by no means hurt them; they will lay hands on the sick, and they will recover" (Mark 16:15-18).*
>
> *Behold, I give you the authority to trample on serpents and scorpions, and over all the power of the enemy, and nothing shall by any means hurt you (Luke 10:19).*

Literally, when I would follow the instruction and mandate of Scripture, doing the works that Jesus said to do, I was told, "You can't do that, you have no authority to do so!"

Being a naïve 20-year-old, I said, "What Bible do you read?!"

I thought we were "Bible-believing" people! I had been taught to be a doer of the word—not just a hearer! (See James 1:22.)

I finally came to understand that, according to their doctrine, I was not "released" to follow and practice the

Word until I had completed their course of studies and become indoctrinated into their denominational doctrine.

Welcome to the world of "religion"! My first thought upon understanding what they meant was, "Did Peter get this memo? If you don't believe these portions of Scripture, why don't you just tear them out of your Bible?"

Peter and all the disciples modeled for us what being a believer in and doer of the Word requires as far as instruction—follow Jesus! Spend time with Him! Do as He says!

I really wanted to make the point to these "learned ones" by handing out scissors in the Bible college for when the professors talk, so you can cut out the Scriptures their doctrine disagrees with. You would come away with an empty book cover!

We must follow the Word, not the professor. Respect them and honor them, but follow the Word. We have got to focus on that which is important, but we were never taught these things. I fumbled through this wilderness of controversy for years trying everything I knew and copying everybody I saw, wanting so much to do what I knew the Word was saying. I was reading and studying everything I could get my hands on because I wanted to do! That was my passion and my heart!

Finally, one day the Lord said, "Sit down! Stop that! I want to share something with you. "

The Lord told me to open the Scripture to the Gospel of Luke and turn to chapter 15. He took me to the parables of the Kingdom.

Parables of the Kingdom: The Prodigal Son

The parable of the lost sheep, the parable of the lost coin, and the parable of the prodigal son—these were where the Lord led me. The Lord said, "Look at this."

In Luke 15, there was a certain man who had two sons. These are parables of the Kingdom, so "that certain man" would be a type of God the Father. The two sons are the Jew and the Gentile, and the younger of the two said, "I want my inheritance now!"

> *Jesus continued: "There was a man who had two sons. The younger one said to his father, 'Father, give me my share of the estate.' So he divided his property between them" (Luke 15:11-12 NIV).*

That's rude! The father was not even dead yet and the son wanted his inheritance? What was the matter with him? And it was even more than that. You see, when the father saw a certain level of maturity at a certain age, he and the son would enter a sandal covenant. This son was demanding that level of covenant. This was totally wrong. But this father, who is a type of God the Father, said OK. He divided their inheritance. He knew what was going to happen. So the son packed up everything and went into a far country. He took his gifts and he wasted them on the gospel of mammon.

> *Not long after that, the younger son got together all he had, set off for a distant country and there squandered his wealth in wild living (Luke 15:13 NIV).*

What is the gospel of mammon? It's kind of like this: "I will give you a $30 word or a $50 word. If you want a good word, I will give you a $100 word, but it is going to cost you." Perry Stone tells the story of a certain individual he was trying to invite to come and minister in his church. The guy he invited sent him a 67-page contract of requirements for him to come and preach the Gospel. That is repugnant and a stench in the nostrils of God.

It breaks my heart, because as we have traveled to many nations of the world, one of the most common things we hear is, "Oh! You are from America, what do you require?" You see, there is a reputation that American Christians come with a certain list of requirements, financial and otherwise, and you have got to do this, that, and the other if you want them to come minister and share Christ. I hate that!

So this young man went and wasted all of his inheritance in riotous living. He was just flippantly treating with disrespect the treasure that God had given him, and he was wasting it. Finally there came a famine in the land.

A famine of what? Well, for that young man, it was a famine of the revelation of the Word and the working of the Word in him. He had so wasted it and his life, and he got into a place of tremendous want and need. So what did he do? He decided to attach himself to the world, so much so that he decided to work for a man of the world. The man said, "Go slop the pigs—that's good for a Jewish boy to do."

After he had spent everything, there was a severe

famine in that whole country, and he began to be in need. So he went and hired himself out to a citizen of that country, who sent him to his fields to feed pigs. He longed to fill his stomach with the pods that the pigs were eating, but no one gave him anything (Luke 15:14-16 NIV).

> When you mix that which is life with that which is the world, that's where you are going to end up—with the pigs.

These Madison Avenue marketing techniques in the church today are a mixture from hell and not from God. You have got to follow the Spirit of God, not the spirit of the world. I am not against demographics if God tells you to study demographics. But we don't embrace these things as a replacement for the Holy Spirit. Tell me how John did with his demographic? John was out in the wilderness, but God brought the people to him. You see, wherever God is moving, people will come. You don't have to move to people to get God to come. You go to where God tells you to be and the people will show up.

So it says that he was so desperate that he was looking for something, anything to eat, and he was even ready to eat the slop that he was feeding to those unclean animals. That is how desperate he had become. Anything the world wanted to feed him he was ready to eat, because he was starving. And then it says he came to himself. The light came on.

> *When he came to his senses, he said, "How many of my father's hired servants have food to spare, and here I am starving to death! I will set out and go back to my father and say to him: Father, I have sinned against heaven and against you. I am no longer worthy to be called your son; make me like one of your hired servants" (Luke 15:17-19 NIV).*

You know what? He said to himself, "In my Father's house, there is plenty to eat, and even the servants eat better than I'm eating. I know what I have to do. I have got to go back to my father and say, 'Father, forgive me. Make me as a servant.'" Look at this—here is the process. He wasted his destiny. He wasted his gifting and was mixing with the world until one day the light came on and he knew what he had to do. "Father, make me," he said. He went from the attitude of "give me" to the attitude of "make me."

The Church in America needs to get away from give me and move toward make me. I am giving you the solution to the frustrations that all of us have gone through at one time or another. "Oh! God! Just give me this. Oh! God! Just give me that." No, that is not the answer! When we say, "Father, make me more like You!" that's spiritual wealth. That's it!

As we walk out this process in our life, the blessings of God overtake us. Remember the old covenant in Deuteronomy 28? If this, then this? If you do what He says, then you will get blessed.

> *Now it shall come to pass, if you diligently obey the voice of the Lord your God, to observe carefully all*

> *His commandments which I command you today, that the Lord your God will set you high above all nations of the earth. And all these blessings shall come upon you and overtake you, because you obey the voice of the Lord your God (Deuteronomy 28:1-2).*

If you don't do what He says, you will get cursed.

> *But it shall come to pass, if you do not obey the voice of the Lord your God, to observe carefully all His commandments and His statutes which I command you today, that all these curses will come upon you and overtake you (Deuteronomy 28:15).*

If you get away from that whole attitude of "give me" and let the attitude of your heart be, "Lord, make me," then all of a sudden you are on the right path, you are going in the right direction, and the blessings of God will begin to shower upon your life. It's the truth.

I was confused for a while because so many of our friends in ministry have seen incredible times of lack for the last few years. It has been so difficult for them. There are just no meetings and the finances have dried up, and so on and so forth. I thought, Really? What's the problem? I began to inquire of God, "Why is this so? What is going on?"

He said, "Process. Get on the right path and My blessings overtake you. It doesn't matter what is going on in the world."

I said, "Yes, Sir."

Being Spirit Led

As I read and re-read the gospels, I noticed an interesting detail about the life and ministry of Jesus compared to the operation and conduct of the modern church. At a word from Jesus, demons would come out. In the church today, we brag about having to wrestle with demons for hours to get a victory.

I noticed that only in a very few instances did Jesus pray for those who came to Him with a sickness or infirmity. He healed them, but it didn't say that He prayed for all of them. He said, "Go in peace, your faith has made you whole" (see Mark 5:34; Luke 7:50; Luke 8:48).

I like the way Jesus operated with no hype, no frills. You know, back in the '70s it seemed like everybody was doing the same thing. "Oh! They need prayer? Get the bottle of oil!" We created a formula out of a principle. We even got that wrong because in the Scriptures it says to call for the elders of the church.

> *Is anyone among you sick? Let them call the elders of the church to pray over them and anoint them with oil in the name of the Lord (James 5:14 NIV).*

According to Hebrew understanding, elders have to be at least 60 years of age, so we kind of messed that one up also. Do you understand that this seems to be a running theme in the church? We take a scripture, we take a facet of revelation, and then we make a formula out of it. When we do that, it equates to witchcraft. You have got to be led of the Spirit.

I love it when Jesus encountered the blind man who came to Him in John 9.

> As he went along, he saw a man blind from birth. His disciples asked him, "Rabbi, who sinned, this man or his parents, that he was born blind?" "Neither this man nor his parents sinned," said Jesus, "but this happened so that the works of God might be displayed in him. As long as it is day, we must do the works of him who sent me. Night is coming, when no one can work. While I am in the world, I am the light of the world." After saying this, he spit on the ground, made some mud with the saliva, and put it on the man's eyes. "Go," he told him, "wash in the Pool of Siloam" (this word means "Sent"). So the man went and washed, and came home seeing (John 9:1-7 NIV).

Jesus spat in the dirt and made mud, then said to the man, "Come here." When I read that I said to the Lord, "Lord! Let me do that! That sounds fun!" And do you know what? The ones who are willing to do that will get healed. So, we have got to be led of the Spirit. I love the fact that Jesus was led of the Spirit, and therefore He says in John 5, "I only do what I see the Father doing, and I only say what I hear the Father saying."

> *Jesus gave them this answer: "Very truly I tell you, the Son can do nothing by himself; he can do only what he sees his Father doing, because whatever the Father does the Son also does" (John 5:19 NIV).*

That's why at the Pool of Bethesda He healed just one, because that's all God told Him to do.

You know, it doesn't look good for your ministry if only one person gets healed. Well, your reputation doesn't mean a whole bunch to God. If you want a reputation in God, follow Jesus and get His reputation. That's how Jesus batted a thousand. He only did what He was told. I love that we should only do what we see the Father do, so I have tried to conform my life to that. It has been so interesting, especially in Asia. Asians love the prophetic. If they know you prophesy, you will be inundated for weeks on end with nonstop requests from everybody who wants a prophetic word. When I ministered there, I had to tell them to stop it! I told them, "I am not your soothsayer and I am not your psychic hotline!"

That's how Jesus batted a thousand. He only did what He was told.

They told me, "But we want a word!"

I said, "Take the Word of God as your word and walk in it." They had made an idol of prophecy.

We see these types of things all over the world. There are different regions that have different inclinations, but do people really understand it when we say, "Just go to Jesus"? We have to realize that we are all in process. Everybody wants a quick and easy solution. Would you like to know the quick and easy solution? OK, here it is. Die! This is what Paul did every day. Paul died daily.

> *I protest by your rejoicing which I have in Christ Jesus our Lord, I die daily (1 Corinthians 15:31 KJV).*

How do you hear God? Well, you shut up and listen. Most people continue on in prayer without giving God a place to answer. When people ask, "Why is it God never talks to me?" I say, "Well, He was just about to, but you left." I am also talking about myself, of course. I learned all these things through experience and by God correcting me, so I am just being honest with you. Do you find yourself also thinking, "I never hear Him"? That's because you don't shut up and listen. The fact is we are always talking. You know, for 30 years or so of my 44 years, I would pray and give God some of the most amazing, creative ideas on how to answer my prayers. Man, I was waxing pretty good there for a while. Not one time did He answer them in that way. He just didn't take any suggestion I ever gave Him. I couldn't understand it until one day I finally got it.

He is God and I am not! We have to quit trying to tell God how to answer our prayers. I am a slow learner too, but I did get there eventually and it changed our lives again. So we have to understand that it is about process.

Remember the key in the word name. This is a key to unlock your destiny. Consider the story about Jacob and Jabbok in Genesis 32. Jacob was a man who stole his birthright from Esau. His mother helped him. It had already been prophesied that the younger would rule over the elder, but they decided they were going to help God. So they plotted, and they stole the birthright. Esau, of course, was in a rage, and so Jacob had to run off. He cheated Esau, and he got cheated himself. He reaped what he sowed. He had to work a lot of years, but then his son was born to carry on the legacy, the destiny that was foretold. So there he was—something shifted in him and he knew that he had better get serious. We read about it starting in verse twenty-two:

> *And he arose that night and took his two wives, his two female servants, and his eleven sons, and crossed over the ford of Jabbok. He took them, sent them over the brook, and sent over what he had. Then Jacob was left alone; and a Man wrestled with him until the breaking of day. Now when He saw that He did not prevail against him, He touched the socket of his hip; and the socket of Jacob's hip was out of joint as He wrestled with him. And He said, "Let Me go, for the day breaks." But he said, "I will not let You go unless You bless me!" So He said to him, "What is your name?" He said, "Jacob." And He said, "Your name shall no longer be called Jacob, but Israel; for you have struggled with God and with men, and have prevailed" (Genesis 32:22).*

But here we find Jacob. He decided that he had to get serious, and he sent his family and all of his servants across the ford of Jabbok, and he stayed at Jabbok all night and wrestled there.

Contending for Your Blessing

He meant business, and there was God wrestling with him, and He said, "Let Me go, Jacob, the day is about to dawn."

"I am not going to let You go until You bless me."

"Jacob, let Me go!"

"I am not going to let You go until You bless me."

He said, "Fine!" Now you are a cripple." What kind of a blessing is that!?

That night Jacob got up and took his two wives, his two female servants and his eleven sons and crossed the ford of the Jabbok. After he had sent them across the stream, he sent over all his possessions. So Jacob was left alone, and a man wrestled with him till daybreak. When the man saw that he could not overpower him, he touched the socket of Jacob's hip so that his hip was wrenched as he wrestled with the man. Then the man said, "Let me go, for it is daybreak. " But Jacob replied, "I will not let you go unless you bless me." The man asked him, "What is your name?"

"Jacob," he answered.

> *Then the man said, "Your name will no longer be Jacob, but Israel, because you have struggled with God and with humans and have overcome" (Genesis 32:22-28 NIV).*

So what kind of a blessing is that?! Here is the spiritual wealth: "No longer can you rely upon your own strength. Now you have to rely upon Me." That's what it took in his life. Jacob was always doing things with his own strength and in his own wisdom. Now he couldn't keep going in his own direction. But Jacob still said, "I am not going to let You go."

The Lord said, "Fine! What is your character?"

And Jacob, in this place of being transparently empty and in this place of brokenness, this is what he said: "I am a heel-catcher, supplanter, and deceiver. I am a used camel salesman."

And the Lord said, "No more. From now on, your character will be Prince with God, one who rules as God." God changed his character to fulfill his destiny!

All throughout Scripture, this is how it works. It doesn't sound too exciting because everybody wants the flashy stuff! But this is how you get to the flashy stuff. This is the foundation that everything is built upon. What I want to release to you here in this revelation is that this is the foundation. You have got to get this. Most Christians want the spectacular, and they neglect the foundation of the supernatural. Did you know that Jesus' 30 years of preparation for three and a half years of ministry were supernatural? Thirty years of sinless existence, submitting Himself to tutors until the time appointed by the Father. That was completely supernatural.

Engaging the Normal Supernatural Life

There are spectacular things that God does, but the foundation of your life should be a supernatural walk with God, not a flash-in-the-pan experience once in a while. That is supernatural. We have had it backwards again because of our flesh. We want to look good. Well, do you know what? God doesn't care what it looks like. I am telling you that your reputation is something that God is going to kill. Yes, He is going to kill it. You have got to become of no reputation.

But made himself of no reputation, and took upon him the form of a servant, and was made in the likeness of men (Philippians 2:7 KJV).

I have studied this for over ten years. Jesus said the works that He did, we can do also. We say, "Oh good! I want to heal the sick and I want to raise the dead and I want to..."

Very truly I tell you, whoever believes in me will do the works I have been doing, and they will do even greater things than these, because I am going to the Father (John 14:12 NIV).

Well, that's good. But here was His first work: He divested Himself of Heaven, of glory; He came to earth as a servant. He submitted Himself to tutors. For the joy that was set before Him, He endured the Cross.

Oh! I don't want that part.

Fixing our eyes on Jesus, the pioneer and perfecter of faith. For the joy set before him he endured the cross, scorning its shame, and sat down at the right hand of the throne of God (Hebrews 12:2 NIV).

I definitely don't want that one. When he was reviled and persecuted, He didn't say anything.

The five-fold ministry is in order. Do you understand? That's the work of Jesus. Too many Christians just want the flash. You will not have the flash without the submission. It doesn't work. Lying signs and wonders come easy. Quality comes through a process of brokenness in your life that brings eternal results.

Translation by Faith

This translation by faith that we teach, the work that Enoch is doing in the world today, and what God is releasing now to this generation requires two things. You will be the Bride of Christ to walk in this, and you will understand the foundation of Christ-like character. You will have these foundations in your life or you will not walk in it. Now, there is a process also in this. It's a process that first starts with dreams, then is manifested in the spirit, and then physically. You know that God will take you a certain distance, but you have to engage the process of the Spirit of perfection that wants to cause you to become other than the nominal Christian we have always been.

> Let's get the foundation solid because we are about to launched into the character of Christ.

That is why we are a people of hunger and passion. I want to encourage you with this. You wouldn't have a hunger and passion if God didn't put it in you, and He didn't put it in you to frustrate you but to cause you to move forward into that fullness-of-time destiny that is yours. He started the work; He is going to complete it, and so my message of this hour and this year is this: Let's get the foundation solid because we are about to launched into the character of Christ.

The Year of Isaiah 60

Arise, shine, for your light has come, and the glory of the Lord rises upon you. See, darkness covers the earth and thick darkness is over the peoples, but the Lord rises upon you and his glory appears over you. Nations will come to your light, and kings to the brightness of your dawn (Isaiah 60:1-3 NIV).

It's time to get the foundation down. Well, what about those who have not even begun? Can I tell you a secret? God can do in a moment what would take you a lifetime. And just calling on Him, "Father, help!" is good because when you are willing, He is your able. That is covenant. He will give you His strength for your weakness. That's covenant!

Let's get the foundation solid because we are about to launched into the character of Christ.

Christ-Like Character

In Exodus it says:

And the Lord said, "I will cause all my goodness to pass in front of you, and I will proclaim my name, the Lord, in your presence. I will have mercy on whom I will have mercy, and I will have compassion on whom I will have compassion" (Exodus 33:19 NIV).

He is going to proclaim the character, the honor, the

authority, the magnificence, and all that God is. This is what He proclaimed before Moses. Basically, in essence (and I will paraphrase this for you) what He said in the Hebrew is this: "Listen, no human being of Adamic DNA can see Me face to face and live." That was before the Cross—Moses was still walking in Adamic DNA. So God said, "What I am going to do is hide you in the cleft of the rock until I walk by, and then you can see Me. In that position of seeing My glory, you are going to see from the beginning of creation all the way up until now."

That is what the Hebrew says, and that is why Moses could write the Book of Genesis. In that experience he saw from creation up until that moment. That is the glory! Arise! Shine! For your light is come, and the glory! We have to understand that there is no time or space with God. He was, is, and always will be right now. Past, present, and future is all right now with God. This is something that I will also share more about in upcoming chapters.

That is how translation by faith works, by the way. So, intrinsic to the character of the Lord is His glory. And if we want these experiences we must cultivate the character. In Leviticus 22:32, it says not to profane His holy character by profaning His name.

> *Do not profane my holy name, for I must be acknowledged as holy by the Israelites. I am the Lord, who made you holy (Leviticus 22:32 NIV).*

We could really cover a lot of ground with this, but basically it is talking about neglecting the process of tutoring of the

Spirit that causes you to become like Him. Refusing to grow up and adhering to a religious system rather than a relational revelation.

The Renewed Covenant

> *After this manner therefore pray ye: Our Father which art in heaven, Hallowed be thy name. Thy kingdom come, Thy will be done in earth, as it is in heaven. Give us this day our daily bread. And forgive us our debts, as we forgive our debtors. And lead us not into temptation, but deliver us from evil: For thine is the kingdom, and the power, and the glory, for ever. Amen (Matthew 6:9-13 KJV).*

Understand that His name is His character. So this conveys, "Our Father in Heaven, hallowed be Your character!" We are saying, "Father, Your character is holy, and I choose today to see it as holy. Hallowed be Your character." And I have already shared that in Matthew 7 Jesus tells us about those who prophesied in His character and didn't know Him:

> *Many will say to me on that day, "Lord, Lord, did we not prophesy in your name and in your name drive out demons and in your name perform many miracles?" Then I will tell them plainly, "I never knew you. Away from me, you evildoers!" (Matthew 7:22-23 NIV)*

There has been no character. Is this making sense to you? In Matthew it says the Gentiles will trust in His name or in His character:

> *And in his name shall the Gentiles trust (Matthew 12:21 KJV).*

When people see the character of Christ in you, there is an immediate response of the Spirit because they see something other than religion or the natural world. They see something different in you when they see the character of Christ, because when you have the character of Christ it exudes out of you. You begin to manifest certain realms or aspects of the Spirit that you never get through prayer. It just starts flowing out of you.

Jesus stood on the Island of Gennesaret and the demons came and fell at His feet. Why? Because at the character of Jesus, every knee bows and every tongue confesses He is Lord.

> *That at the name of Jesus every knee should bow, of things in heaven, and things in earth, and things under the earth; and that every tongue should confess that Jesus Christ is Lord, to the glory of God the Father (Philippians 2:10-11 KJV).*

When you come in this manner, you don't even have to preach, you just come with the manifest presence and character of God, and spontaneously the realm of the natural begins to act up, and then the spiritual. I am telling you something important here. This is what God wants to do. This is the Charles Finney anointing on steroids. This is what God wants to release to you. This is what He has had us walking out for the last ten years. We have practiced this as our lifestyle. How do you practice that? We agree with

Him every day. When you come in agreement you declare, "Father, Your character is the most important thing in my life. Make me like You." He will honor a prayer like that.

During a conference a few years ago, I was asking the Lord, "Lord, when are we going to start walking in the manifestation of all these things?" He told us to go ahead! "OK..." I thought, "so what do I do then?" He said to ask if there was anybody in the room who had pain in their body, and so I did.

Many hands went up, but there was one guy going, "Oh! Oh! Oh! Oh!"

I asked him, "OK, what is the problem?"

He said, "For three years I have had excruciating pain in my heels. Medical science can't diagnose it and nothing works, not shots or anything. Every morning I wake up and I am in agony, and I weep for the first two hours as I just loosen it up, and by the end of the day it is just bearable and then it starts the cycle again."

I asked him, "What is going to happen? What is going to happen to you when we pray?" I said, "How are you going to know you are healed?"

He said, "Tomorrow when I wake up there will be no pain."

I said, "Brother, go in peace. Your faith has made you whole."

And of course, as everyone watched this the church was going, "That's it?" This was an African church, and this was a fun experience for me. They were very boisterous and I loved their worship. We had a blast with these people, but they were kind of wondering about all of this. The next day I was again up there speaking, and I saw this same guy with the heel problem come in late. I didn't even ask him; I just handed him the mic and said, "Tell them what happened."

He said, "I woke up this morning and there has been no pain. I am healed!" Praise God!

I asked the Lord, and He told me, "That's how you do this. Let My character be the preeminent thing, not your gifting." Let me say that again. Let My character become the preeminent thing in your life, not gifting. Because if you walk in My character, the gifting takes care of itself, and where My character is, there is My authority.

So we practice this all over the world, and we see instant miracles all the time, but you have got to follow the leading of the Spirit. In the book of John it says, "Whatever you ask in My name, that I will do" (John 14:13). Oops! Whatever you ask with Christ-like character, He will do it. Where two or more of you are gathered together with Christ-like character, there He is in the midst. So many churches just wave the banner, the religious banner—Jesus! Jesus! Jesus! And do you know what? There is apostasy and perversion all around, but they still used that terminology. That's not what it was all about. Where two or more are gathered together with Christ-like character, that is where He is. And if you have His character, you won't ask amiss because you are

> Let My character be the preeminent thing in your life, not the gifting

not going to consume it upon your lusts because you can't. You are like Him.

Manifesting the Character of Christ

I have manifested thy name unto the men which thou gavest me out of the world: thine they were, and thou gavest them me; and they have kept thy word (John 17:6 KJV).

Jesus said, "I have manifested Your character to the men whom You have given me out of the world. I have manifested Your name; I have manifested Your character."

God has given every one of you a sphere of influence. You are called to manifest His character to that sphere of influence. Those are the ones God has given you! Whoever calls upon the character of the Lord shall be saved. You can come up with your own examples, just get that in your mind.

> *He that hath an ear, let him hear what the Spirit saith unto the churches; To him that overcometh will I give to eat of the hidden manna, and will give him a white stone, and in the stone a new name written, which no man knoweth saving he that receiveth it (Revelation 2:17 KJV).*

In the book of Revelation it says, "To him who overcomes." Overcomes what?

Those who hang on until the end? No. You have things to overcome every single day. Every day. To him who overcomes He will give some of the hidden manna. Every day you can overcome and receive fresh manna from Heaven, fresh revelation, fresh strength and insight. He says He will give you a white stone, and on the stone a new character, which no one knows except you. So what am I saying? You can't share it? No. Let me define this in Hebrew terms.

There is a process to which everybody is called. Now, your innermost being, your heart, only you and God know, and you don't even know most of it, but God does. You know a process; you know the things you have overcome, the difficulties you have faced, the struggles you have had, the victories you have won. Only you know that in complete harmony with God. So the character that He develops from that whole process, only you and He will know. That facet of His character only you and He will know. Nobody else is going to understand the complexity of how you got to that place, only you and God alone. That's what this white stone with a new name means.

It doesn't mean that you can't say, "My name is Fred." No, you are still Fred. That's not what He is saying. He is talking about the process of the character that He has developed in you and what that character reflects of Him.

God Desires to Develop Your Character

In ancient times, certain kinds of stones carried significant or special meaning. In John's day, a white stone was used in the judicial process, and it meant not guilty—pure, holy, and not guilty. This is the Word of the Lord for you. God wants to develop your character so you can see the conclusion of the matter of His destiny for you in your own life. What He has for His people in this hour, there is no language yet able to frame proper terminology to express it. I have seen it in Heaven and I have seen it begin to spark on the earth, but we haven't seen anything yet. It says in the Scripture that if everything that Jesus said and did were written, the world couldn't contain the volumes of the books.

Do you think maybe there are some things Jesus has reserved for this generation that no other generation has seen? I know there are, but we will not walk in them without His character. If we walked in those powers of the age to come that He is talking about, it would destroy a fleshly individual. But if you have the character of Christ, you will give all glory to God.

A Prophetic Gesture

A prophetic gesture is an action that we take physically as a step of faith to cause or believe something will happen either spiritually or physically. It is an act of putting action to our faith, much like the man with the withered hand in Matthew 12. He was told to "Stretch forth your hand." He did so as a step of faith and his hand was restored.

> *Then saith he to the man, Stretch forth thine hand. And he stretched it forth; and it was restored whole, like as the other (Matthew 12:13 KJV).*

There are many examples in Scripture, but the main idea is that we are putting action with our faith and believing for God to move.

As I mentioned, there are white stones that the Lord desires to give His children at this time. There are angels with white stones, and they are prepared to give them to those who will receive from the Lord. As a prophetic promise for you, God is going to give you that stone. There is a grace in this season that comes with this, and although many are in a different place, God is doing an accelerated work. If you study the seventh day in the Scriptures, you will see it is a day of visitation and it is His custom to visit the temple. You are the temple and He will do in a moment what you can't do in a lifetime as He visits the temple.

So, as a prophetic gesture please put this book down for a moment and stand up. Hold out your right hand as though to receive something. (The right hand speaks of greater strength and greater blessing.)

Now as I pray this prayer of release, faith, and activation, and as you read it, just allow God to place the stone in your hand and receive it by faith.

A Prayer

Father, now let those ministering angels place that white stone into their hands, and as You are imparting this truth and imparting this revelation, Father, I thank You for visitation and acceleration in their individual and corporate life, that they would progress swiftly now into the place of destiny that You have called them to. Lord, it is not going to be the logical, reasoning mind that figures this out. Your Spirit and their spirit—I can hear their spirit shouting yes and amen! And Father, Your Spirit is saying yes and amen! And so we agree together with You. You are going to do what we could never do. I thank You for covenant; I thank You for the grace that You are releasing now and the mercy that You are helping us in our infirmities, Father. Bless Your people, Father; even this very night, begin to visit them in their sleep or awaken them and visit them face to face. Father, start this process and bring it quickly to pass, and I will bless You for that, Most High. I love You, Father.

The Word of the Lord

Eye has not seen and ear has not heard, neither has it entered into the heart of man what I have prepared for those who truly love Me. But in this hour of My grace, I am opening the eyes, I am opening the ears, and I am opening My people's hearts to receive of Me that which I have withheld from past generations because that has been reserved for this generation. I have chosen you; you are My Beloved. I choose this day to release to you these covenantal blessings that you have not understood and have never ever had it enter into your heart to ask for, but I am releasing a blessing to you that you will not be able to contain. It will overflow your life, it will overflow your family, it will touch the lives of many around you, and many who are in the valley of decision will see this overflow and come running to it and be caught up into My presence and know that I am God of a truth. For I tell you what I have prepared for you will be so exponentially other than anything you have ever expressed or desired that it will take a people who know My heart and know My voice to be able to receive and walk in it.

I release this word of the Lord to you right now.

5

TAKING STEPS OF FAITH

There are multitudes of angels and they come with purpose. Sometimes, but not often, angels will come to gaze into the mystery of what God is unveiling in us. Sometimes they come because they are going to participate in what the Lord wants to do, and this is one of those times. As we enter into the revelation that is being released in these pages, they are with us to minister to and for us, the heirs of salvation.

Over the years it has been very interesting to see different groups of angels come into the meetings as we have ministered in various places around the world. The angels come in and they minister, and there have been many unusual manifestations that are hard to describe or define. There have been unusual things that happen in the lives of people, and right now we are in one of those times. I was asking the Lord what revelation He wants to share with you here in these pages. I could really go a hundred different directions, but He told me start with this.

The Hand of God

A few years ago the Lord opened my eyes to something that even to this day causes me to go "tilt." The fleshly mind cannot grasp the weight of what God showed me, and I ponder on it all the time, I meditate on it, and yet I still find myself going "tilt." In Isaiah 40:12 it says that the Lord has measured the waters in the hollow of His hand and He has measured the heavens with a span. A span is from the little finger to the end of your thumb.

> *Who hath measured the waters in the hollow of his hand, and meted out heaven with the span, and comprehended the dust of the earth in a measure, and weighed the mountains in scales, and the hills in a balance? (Isaiah 40:12 KJV)*

Other passages of Scripture in other versions say that everything that He created fits in the span of His hand. Do you know the universe and the galaxies are ever expanding? And it all fits in the span of His hand. And then in Psalms He says He gives you dominion over all the works of His hand.

> *Thou madest him to have dominion over the works of thy hands; thou hast put all things under his feet (Psalms 8:6).*

Now wrap your mind around that one. Everything He creates fits in the span of His hand, and He gives you dominion over all the works of it. Tilt! And you know, if you look at that you understand how some of the things that we contend with every day are so petty and insignificant. We have got to get a sense of the bigger picture, because what God has invested in you is so far beyond what you can imagine. I meditated on that for a few years, and one time as I was in my office praying, all of a sudden I was caught up into paradise, and I saw the Father.

It is not often you get to see the Father, but I saw Him from behind. I have never seen into His face, at least not yet. How do you know it is the Father? Because you are in Heaven and you instantly know. And as I was there, He was walking around Paradise and was looking at His creation, and of course I was curious. I was looking at His hand. "What have you got in Your hand, Lord?" And then finally I was able to see—I could feel His feelings. He was almost smiling and kind of laughing at me. And I looked into His hand and I saw all of creation, and it just overwhelmed me! And I saw that it was alive, and it was worshiping Him, and it was amazing, like some kind of heavenly CD.

> There is nothing in the universe that is bigger than God, and you are in Him. You are in Him!

I don't know how that all works. It was just the worshiping of God because that's what all of creation does. And I was looking at it and it was expanding, yet it never went beyond His hand, and I was just mystified and in awe. He smiled and turned to me, and with His left hand He grabbed my right hand, and He put it in my hand. Yes, He put all of creation in my hand. He said, "You tell My people it is time they walked in this."

There are many days I just look at my hand and I remember this and think, "What am I not doing today to realize the truth of what He has expressed?" It is baffling to me sometimes. There is nothing in the universe that is bigger than God, and you are in Him. You are in Him! Now, if you will just start meditating on these things for a while you will begin to walk differently. It changed how Reshma and I both saw things.

Speaking to the Rain

> Now Elijah the Tishbite, from Tishbe in Gilead, said to Ahab, "As the Lord, the God of Israel, lives, whom I serve, there will be neither dew nor rain in the next few years except at my word" (1 Kings 17:1 NIV).

Reshma is from Fiji, and there was a sweet lady there by the name of Opal Moore. She is not there anymore, she is living in Hawaii now. Opal is 85 or 86 now, still preaching and still pastoring, still starting churches. She was in Fiji at the time of this miraculous event, and Opal is the reason I first got invited to go there. This time, Reshma and I went back to visit after we had been married for a few years, and we walked into her home, and it was just pouring torrents of rain. I asked her, "So how is it going? How has the weather been?" Because as you probably know, Fiji is a tropical climate.

She said, "Oh! It has been miserable; it has been raining so much we can't even go out and do anything!"

Then out of my spirit (not my head), I said, "Well, what are you doing about it?"

I was a bit taken aback by the word that came out of my own mouth. And she asked me, "What do you mean?"

At that point, Reshma and I grabbed hands and we said, "In the name of Jesus, rain, you stop until we give you permission to rain again." The rain then cleared up, and it didn't rain for two weeks. You see, that was practicing the revelation. It is good to have a revelation, but unless you practice you don't become proficient. You don't need head knowledge. You need activation, and it seems that everybody wants somebody else to activate them. Can I give you a piece of revelation? You have been given enough to activate it yourself. Do something with what God has given you!

This is why I like prophetic gestures. Somebody will always say, "Well, that looks foolish!" Good. Kill some more of that flesh and ego and step into God's reality. It is OK to be a fool in the eyes of man. That will make you wise in the eyes of God.

> *But the natural man receiveth not the things of the Spirit of God: for they are foolishness unto him: neither can he know them, because they are spiritually discerned (1 Corinthians 2:14 KJV).*

So the last couple days of our trip over there, we stayed at a resort hotel just to take a break, and we were in the swimming pool and having a good time. And Reshma said to me, "Oh! Do you think we should let it rain now?"

And I went, "Oh! Yeah, I guess we'd better." So we said, "Rain, OK, you can come back." Within 20 minutes it came—lightning and thunder, and we had to get out of the pool!

I'm not sharing this with you so that you might think that we are something special. I pray you understand that.

I share this so that you might look at the Word of God and realize that this is for you to do also. We have got to practice this stuff so that when the world sees you, they really see something that can change their lives. Do they really see Jesus, or do they only see a chameleon? I have some news for you. You are not going to get to remain a chameleon much longer, not if you are hungry for God. The raging of Satan at the end of the age is not against mediocre Christianity—do you understand that? He is going to rage against saints who are standing on the Word and walking in the maturity and in the promises of God. Those are the ones he can't stand; the rest he has no issue with.

Well I, for one, am going to make him work. I am going to make him sweat. For a number of years the Lord has been teaching me about light. I going to give you a preamble here. If you have read one of my books called Gazing Into Glory, you know that back in the year 2001 the Lord started teaching me about translocation, translation by faith, and how to go from one geographic area to another instantly by the spirit. Back then it was not only a revelation that no one else was sharing, it was get the "white jacket" for that guy! It used to make Reshma nervous because automatically everyone would think you were weird. I said, "Yeah! I am!"

But this walk and revelation has been a progression for us, because even as the Lord has been gracious to me and has given me revelation, it is a line upon line and precept upon precept kind of thing, here a little and there a little. It wasn't just like boom and you got it. I don't care what you have gotten by revelation, that's not even an nth degree of the revelation that comes or the revelation that's available.

We are going to be discovering mysteries for eternity. We are never going to exhaust the revelation in that. And so the Lord has built upon this for years and He has given experiences and expressions and activations in other lives also and it has been awesome, but I had my focus in the wrong place for a while. Because I was looking at Phillip, and I was looking at some of these other accounts of translation in Scripture, I said, "God, this was physical."

> This current natural reality that we experience is a dark reflection of the reality of eternity.

Yes, some of it was and some of it wasn't. He said, and I am going to paraphrase it, "Well, are you a human being or are you a spirit being?"

When I was born again, I became a man of the spirit who lived in an earthly body. Before I was born again, I was a human being looking for a spirit. That is how many get demon possessed or follow the dark side. The Lord said, "Identify with who I say you are, not who you think you are." In other words, I am spirit; I have a soul that connects my spirit to the natural realm, and I dwell in a mortal body. But I am a spirit. He said that when we have spiritual experiences, visions, or dreams or there are times that we are actually there, that is the true reality, more than this dark realm called the natural world. This current natural reality that we experience is a dark reflection of the reality of eternity.

You Bring the Glory

I told the Lord OK. I got my focus back onto spirit rather than focusing on the flesh moving in spiritual things. Once I got that, He started teaching me about who we really are. You are a being of light and you were created in His image. I began to study that revelation and meditate on it. We'd had a very busy schedule for a lot of years. I think a few years there we were only home two months out of twelve.

One time, Reshma had stayed home, but I was in Maryland ministering. I was really ready to go home, but a pastor affiliated with our ministry said, "Hey, would you come over to our church and minister? We are going to dedicate our new facility and ordain people."

I said, "No, I need to go home. I really need a break."

But this pastor continued, "We really want you to come."

I said, "Look, I don't need to speak. You have already got your lineup in place; there's no reason for me to come."

In the midst of all this the Lord spoke to me. The Lord said, "Be quiet and go.

And so I said, "Oh! OK." I then told him, "OK, Brother, the Lord said I am supposed to come."

He said, "Oh! Good! We are going to have you speak." I protested that I didn't need to speak; I just wanted to rest. "No, no," he said. He wanted me to speak. He said, "The speaker the first night is a friend of ours from Africa. Bishop Newaka is a powerful man of God, and he wants you to speak before he does." I insisted that I didn't want to take his time. He said, "No, he is asking for you to speak."

I just kept arguing, and the Lord finally said, "Just be quiet and say yes." The Lord has never talked to me like that. Finally, the pastor said they would give me 15 minutes.

I said, "OK. That's fine, I can say hello and greet everyone, but why do you want me to speak for 15 minutes?"

He responded, "Because you bring the glory."

In 15 minutes?! I said, "God, what are You doing? You are setting me up to look even more foolish than I usually am." With all of that settled, I was in the hotel room praying, "What are You doing, Lord? This is so weird. Fifteen minutes? Fifteen minutes to bring the glory?" This was an African pastor also, so they are very organized and they have got a program they want to follow. I am not against programs if it is God, and so I was praying, and all of a sudden I found myself standing in the realm of the Spirit.

Removing the Garment of Flesh

I was standing in this place in the realm of the spirit, and I was looking around to see what the Lord wanted to show me. The Lord said, "Take off that garment." Have you ever seen the movie Superman? When Clark Kent "becomes" Superman, he pulls his shirt apart, exposing his true identity with the "S" symbol on his chest. So, like Superman, I pulled away my garment of flesh just like Superman did with his natural garments. When I did that what was exposed was light! I was light, and I gasped! The Lord said, "No. Take the garment off." So I removed the garment of flesh and I was standing there as a being of light, and I was completely in awe. I looked behind me and there was this raggedy garment of flesh laying there! And the Lord said, "This is who I say you are. This is what you are when you are born again. You are a being of light." He told me to start seeing myself as a being of light. I was completely shocked, and then I found myself back in my room.

I removed the garment of flesh and I was standing there as a being of light

Immediately I opened my Bible. I had a new Bible then, and it just fell open. I don't pursue seemingly random openings of the Bible—that is not how I pursue God—but it opened and went immediately to Mark chapter 9, the Mount of Transfiguration. He said, "You know that you can do this by faith."

The Transfiguration

After six days Jesus took Peter, James and John with him and led them up a high mountain, where they were all alone. There he was transfigured before them. His clothes became dazzling white, whiter than anyone in the world could bleach them. And there appeared before them Elijah and Moses, who were talking with Jesus.

Peter said to Jesus, "Rabbi, it is good for us to be

> here. Let us put up three shelters—one for you, one for Moses and one for Elijah." (He did not know what to say, they were so frightened.)
>
> Then a cloud appeared and covered them, and a voice came from the cloud: "This is my Son, whom I love. Listen to him!"
>
> Suddenly, when they looked around, they no longer saw anyone with them except Jesus.
>
> As they were coming down the mountain, Jesus gave them orders not to tell anyone what they had seen until the Son of Man had risen from the dead. They kept the matter to themselves, discussing what "rising from the dead" meant.
>
> And they asked him, "Why do the teachers of the law say that Elijah must come first?"
>
> *Jesus replied, "To be sure, Elijah does come first, and restores all things. Why then is it written that the Son of Man must suffer much and be rejected? But I tell you, Elijah has come, and they have done to him everything they wished, just as it is written about him" (Mark 9:2-13 NIV).*

I closed the Bible and said, "Yes, Lord, I know that, but..." Then I just began to meditate about this vision and I said, "Lord, would You give me one more word?" I opened the Bible and this is what He gave me:

> *For God hath not given us the spirit of fear; but of power, and of love, and of a sound mind (2 Timothy 1:7 KJV).*

The Lord said to me, "I have not given you a spirit of fear, but of power, love, and a sound mind." And He told me that this is of grace.

I said, "OK, Lord, what do You want me to tell these people then?"

He said, "Just share with them exactly what you walked through"—the revelation that we had just progressed into.

I arrived that night and the worship was already over and the pastor whispered in my ear, "OK, fifteen minutes. Here you go." So I stood there before the people and shared with them exactly what had happened. It took me nine minutes. I know because I was watching the clock. After I had delivered that word, the presence of God came in and nobody could move. It was the glory of God that fell and it was tangible. The pastor then walked up to me very cautiously, and he said, "Whatever God tells you to do, do it."

I said, "I did," and he didn't know what to do. No one knew what to do in this glory that fell. So he just fell back into the program, and the presence of God lifted. It was a learning curve experience for all of us.

The Lord said, "My presence is not in a multitude of words; it is in obedience to My word. Just do what I tell you to do and you will see My presence manifest wherever you go. But remember this lesson—you are a being of light."

Here is what happens with me when God gives me a revelation like that. I practice every day. Every morning, part of my prayer regimen is that I see myself taking off the garment of flesh and standing there as a being of light, and

I make a declaration in my heart that I am going to walk with the awareness that I am a being of light that day. If you do that, it begins to change your life. You see, you have got to put your faith into action. Faith without works is what? Dead. And if your faith hasn't been used or exercised for a while, that which has been dead for a while "stinketh." So you have got to do something by faith to agree with the word God has given you.

I was called by the Lord at age fourteen, out of Jeremiah 1—a prophet to the nations.

> *The word of the Lord came to me, saying, "Before I formed you in the womb I knew you, before you were born I set you apart; I appointed you as a prophet to the nations" (Jeremiah 1:4-5 NIV).*

Back in the 1970s there was no paradigm for that in the church. Either you would be a missionary or you would be an evangelist, but there was no paradigm for "prophet to the nations." I stumbled through, but God taught me. I didn't have a mentor except for the Holy Ghost, and really, He is the best mentor. And so, when He finally said in 1997, "OK, now I am releasing you into this," I had been a youth pastor, an associate pastor, and I had taught in schools, etc. But He told me that I was going to start traveling. I knew I had to do something by faith.

Now at that point, I barely had enough money to pay attention. I was only occasionally working in IT when there was a big job to be found. I had an apartment and I was just about making the rent payment on it, and I had only $20 in my pocket after that, so I knew I must do something by faith. I already had a passport, so I packed a suitcase and kept it in my closet. I said, "I am ready, God." I responded by faith.

Steps of Faith

One day the Lord said to me, "I want you to go to Fiji." This was in 1998. He said, "I want you go to Fiji and minister."

I said, "OK, Lord." So right away I called the airline. I lived in San Antonio at that time, and I asked them, "How much is a ticket from San Antonio to Los Angeles?" In Los Angeles there was a wholesaler for Fiji travel where, for $210, you could buy a ticket. I told them to hold the ticket for me. I had 72 hours from that time to purchase the ticket. So I got off the phone, and I said, "OK, Lord, now what? I only have $20." He told me to call a man I'd done a little work for. He said there was some money on his books for me. I said, "Really? I didn't know that." So I called this person up and I said, "Hey! Do I have anything on the books there?"

He checked and said, "Yeah! You do! You have got $210." I told him I needed that to go to Fiji. He said, "You can go to Fiji for $210? Can I come?" I said sure!

So I bought the ticket. I landed in LA—and that was as far as I got. I had $20. I called some friends up in the Mojave Desert in a little town called Boron, California ("Boring," California). It is a very small, little nowhere place. I told my friends, "I am nearby, and I am on my way to Fiji. What's going on with you?" I was not specific at all.

They said, "Well, could you come up and do some meetings?" I said agreed, and they drove down two hours to pick me up. I went up there and spent a whole week ministering in this little church. There were more tumbleweeds than there were people, but I had a good time.

One of the things that the Lord taught me when He told me I was going to travel in ministry was, "Don't you ever ask for a thing, don't you ever knock on any door, and don't you ever break your word. If you say you are going, you will go." The Lord has tested me on this. He said, "If you tell a church of ten you are coming, and then a church of a thousand asks you come on the same date, don't you break your word." So that is how I live.

> If you tell a church of ten you are coming, and then a church of a thousand asks you come on the same date, don't you break your word

So the week at this church was over, and they collected a couple of offerings, and it was not enough to get to Fiji. I thought, "Oh! Good! I can go home now! I did what I was supposed to do, Lord." And I was really at peace about that.

The next morning—the day I would have had to fly out, buy the ticket, and fly to Fiji—this pastor came over, a little white-haired lady named Dot. She sat down and we were chatting over coffee. Then she said, "The Lord told me to do this," and she pulled out her purse and started putting down $100 bills.

As she was putting them down, the only thing that went through my mind was, "Oh! Darn it! Now I have to go!"

The couple I was staying with almost fell over. They said, "We have known her for fifty years and she has never done that."

I said, "Well, that figures." So I packed and rushed to the airport and spent over a month in Fiji. I still had $400 left when I got there, so I gave it to a missionary. When I got back home, I still had my original $20. You see, that is an adventure. I have never seen the righteous forsaken or their seed begging for bread (see Ps. 37:25 NIV).

We always put obstacles in our own path, not God's path. You can't build an obstacle big enough for God. We say, "God, if my bills are paid then I will go. If this is right and that is taken care of and…." Stop that! God is not under your authority; you are under His authority. When you recognize that and say, "Yes, Sir," He takes care of everything. I practice my faith. Whatever He shows me, I try to do something by faith to put it into practice, and every day it has changed some things.

Sadhu Sundar Selvaraj

The Lord had been teaching me about this three years earlier. That August, we had our annual conference with a brother by the name of Sadhu Sundar Selvaraj. Brother Sadhu is a good friend, and he is really funny. His father was a Hindu priest, so he wasn't happy when his son got saved at the age of sixteen. Brother Sadhu had started reading some books about some pastors in India who were walking in mystical experiences, seeing the unseen and having encounters with God, and he said, "Lord, I want that." So the Lord took him to Ephesians 1:18:

> *I pray that the eyes of your heart may be enlightened in order that you may know the hope to which he has called you, the riches of his glorious inheritance in his holy people, and his incomparably great power for us who believe (Ephesians 1:18-19 NIV).*

It didn't matter where he was, whether on the bus or wherever he might be, every time he had a free moment he would drop to his knees, in public on the street, and pray that prayer. He would tell the Lord, "Lord, I want this." Within three months, his spiritual eyes were opened, and he has seen in that realm ever since then. Three months! Think about that! I said, "You know, Brother Sadhu, I don't know if I like you anymore. It took me a lot longer than three months." But that is the way God works, and Brother Sadhu now has incredible encounters all of the time.

Brother Sadhu was at our conference, and the first afternoon he came in smiling, and we went into the Green Room to visit. He said, "I had a visitation last night," and began telling us, "Abraham came and talked about this." He is always having these encounters. They are very accurate and it is awesome to listen to him share these encounters and revelations. After sharing about this incredible visitation from Abraham, he said, "Oh! At the end of this visitation with Abraham, before he walked out, he turned and said,

'Oh! And tell Bruce....'" And Brother Sadhu shared a message from Abraham given to him for me!

I said, "Wow! I made the addendum list! And what was that revelation that Abraham had for me? He told me to study light, "because light is a key to what he has been walking out." It was an incredible and confirming message to say the least!

At that point I had not told him about the whole Superman, super-saint thing that I had been instructed to do, with removing the garment of flesh. So I just said thank you. Then in September we were ministering with Neville Johnson and Sadhu in Sydney, Australia. I was there praying and asking the Lord, "Lord, what am I doing here?" I was thinking that maybe I was there to be the water carrier or something, because these guys were the heroes of the faith to me. As I was in my room praying—and I was really praying, "God, help!"—all of a sudden I was in the Spirit again, and I was in a massive cave, and you could see out the front of the cave that the sun was setting. As a child, I used to like the television program Wild Kingdom; it was my favorite show, and I remembered seeing pictures of the sunset going down on the Serengeti with its big red sun. And that is what I saw at the cave, and I knew immediately that it was the end of the age and just prior to the return of Jesus.

I was looking at this scene before me and just marveling at the experience when all of a sudden a man stepped up next to me, and it was Elijah. I had never had an encounter with a saint before, so this was a learning curve for me.

Many in the church would call this necromancy! Right? No, it was not. I didn't call anybody up; he just popped in, and believe me, God is the God of the living, not the dead (see Mark 12:27).

The very first thing I did was ask, "Did Jesus Christ come in the flesh?" I always do this because I don't want to be deceived.

He said, "Of course He did. That is the reason I am here." I responded, "Well, why are you here?"

He said, "The Lord sent me to teach you how a man can go from the natural realm and this life to eternity without seeing death."

I told him, "I am listening."

And he put out his arm and it became light. And he said to me, "Go ahead." I tried to do the same, but nothing at all happened. I tried everything I could to do what he had done, and I could not.

You Are the Key

Elijah laughed at me. He said, "No. Remember what God has already taught you." So I stood there for a minute considering what God had taught me. I held out my arm again and this time it became light. He said, "Good. Keep practicing until it becomes natural, not second nature but first nature, because we are spirit." So I just kept doing it, and after a while he said, "Good! You've got it!" Then he stood in front of me, and he held out a key that was made out of light.

Now, this is another story, but let me backtrack a moment and tell you that I had received this same key three or four years previously during Rosh Hashanah. I knew that this key had to do with portals, gateways, and doorways. I was thinking, "How did you get my key?"

He said, "Put your arm out," and I again extended my arm and it was light. Then he set the key in my hand and it dissolved into me.

I said, "What was that?"

He said, "You are the same frequency of light. Listen now." He said, "You are the key. You are the key. You are beings of light!"

That was another thing that caused my thinking to go "tilt." I had been studying physics—not because I like it but because of the experiences that God had given me, and I needed to understand what He was teaching me. These kinds of experiences from God will definitely cause you or provoke you to a hunger for greater understanding. I learned that light is a frequency and a wall is a frequency. Then Elijah said, "Good. Now, follow me," and He walked right through the wall. I tried to follow him and walked right into the wall. He began laughing again. I can still hear him laughing. I was going ouch! This is what caused me to know that we were in a real place—because I felt it.

You are the same frequency of light. Listen now." He said, "You are the key

He said, "No, remember!" He said to come into agreement with the same frequency at which the wall resonates. When I did, I walked right through it. I had a mantle on and the wall snagged it and jerked me back, pulling me down. It sat me down on the ground, and then Elijah was laughing again! He is such a jolly old character!

I was thinking to myself, "I'm glad I'm bringing you such amusement." But really, there is so much joy in Heaven. There was no pain in any of this.

As far as hanging on to my mantle that caught in the wall, he said, "No, let that go. That's the Second Day mantle you are wearing. It's time for the new mantle."

Arise and Shine!

So we practiced, and the Lord said, "Continue to study, because the day is coming when this will be as natural as breathing." So when I was praying in the New Year, I said, "Lord, what are You saying for 2016?" He said it was the year for Isaiah 60, and I thought wow! Isaiah 60 says Arise! Shine!

Arise, shine, for your light has come, and the glory of the Lord rises upon you. See, darkness covers the earth and thick darkness is over the peoples, but the Lord rises upon you and his glory appears over you. Nations will come to your light, and kings to the brightness of your dawn. Lift up your eyes and look about you: All assemble and come to you; your sons come from afar, and your daughters are carried on the hip. Then you will look and be radiant, your heart will throb and swell with joy ;the wealth on the seas will be brought to you, to you the riches of the nations will come.

Herds of camels will cover your land, young camels of Midian and Ephah. And all from Sheba will come, bearing gold and incense and proclaiming the praise of the Lord. All Kedar's flocks will be gathered to you, the rams of Nebaioth will serve you; they will be accepted as offerings on my altar ,and I will adorn my glorious temple. Who are these that fly along like clouds, like doves to their nests? Surely the islands look to me; in the lead are the ships of Tarshish, bringing your children from afar, with their silver and gold, to the honor of the Lord your God, the Holy One of Israel, for he has endowed you with splendor. Foreigners will rebuild your walls, and their kings will serve you. Though in anger I struck you, in favor I will show you compassion. Your gates will always stand open, they will never be shut, day or night, so that people may bring you the wealth of the nations—their kings led in triumphal procession. For the nation or kingdom that will not serve you will perish; it will be utterly ruined.

The glory of Lebanon will come to you, the juniper, the fir and the cypress together, to adorn my sanctuary; and I will glorify the place for my feet. The children of your oppressors will come bowing before you all who despise you will bow down at your feet and will call you the City of the Lord, Zion of the Holy One of Israel. Although you have been forsaken and hated, with no one traveling through,

I will make you the everlasting pride and the joy of all generations. You will drink the milk of nations and be nursed at royal breasts. Then you will know that I, the Lord, am your Savior, your Redeemer, the Mighty One of Jacob. Instead of bronze I will bring you gold and silver in place of iron. Instead of wood I will bring you bronze, and iron in place of stones. I will make peace your governor and well-being your ruler. No longer will violence be heard in your land, nor ruin or destruction within your borders, but you will call your walls Salvation and your gates Praise. The sun will no more be your light by day, nor will the brightness of the moon shine on you, for the Lord will be your everlasting light and your God will be your glory. Your sun will never set again and your moon will wane no

> *more; the Lord will be your everlasting light and your days of sorrow will end.*
>
> *Then all your people will be righteous and they will possess the land forever. They are the shoot I have planted, the work of my hands, for the display of my splendor. The least of you will become a thousand the smallest a mighty nation. I am the Lord; in its time I will do this swiftly (Isaiah 60 NIV).*

You see, that first word is very important. It is a command that we do something. Arise! Do something! So how do you do something? You arise, you stand up! Do something. Then shine! You come into agreement with who you are. I am a being of light and so are you! Arise and shine!

A few years ago in Boston, we were ministering in a historic church, and the worship seemed to be going nowhere. I mean it was hitting the roof and bouncing back down, and it was like holy moly! I had never been in a more difficult place to break through. And the pastor came out after an hour and said, "We are just not breaking through. What do we do now?"

I said, "Just keep worshiping! You don't need to hear me! We need to hear God!" So we just kept worshiping. I am not a person who is given to fleshly demonstrations. That's not who I am. If God moves on me, I will do whatever He says, but I am not looking for attention. But all of a sudden, as I was just standing there after hours of this, my body started vibrating with the power of God. "That's interesting!" I thought. "What is that?" And when I asked that, immediately the back wall opened up and I saw Paradise. I saw the Throne of God. There was an angel standing at this portal, and I saw the River of God come and fall into the room, and when it did worship broke out, and then we broke through.

I saw the Sea of Glass before the Throne of God, and there were millions of people there worshiping. It was interesting to watch because whole rows of people would go up and down like a sign wave. So you would see different levels of the worship—it was like a crescendo of a note. Not one of them was opening their mouth, but still this amazing symphony of worship was pouring forth. I was looking at this, and then I noticed something—I realized that there was a sound coming out of me! I said, "Lord, what is this?" The Lord explained to me that the way I have read the Bible, Psalms 22:3 says, "But thou art holy, O thou that inhabitest the praises of Israel" (KJV), but the original language says I inhabit My people who are praise.

Many times in worship, I will just stand there and release worship. Not with my physical body, but I let the resonating frequency of worship and praise that I am join the symphony of Heaven, and it is transforming. It is the same thing. You are a being of light—shine! How do you shine? I see it. When you practice, you have got to see. Let me explain this to you. Remember in 1 Kings 17, 18, and 19 the story of Elijah? Elijah is one of my heroes because, as you may know, this is an Elijah generation. The fact that he showed up just made it all the better.

Elijah and the Brook at Cherith

> Now Elijah the Tishbite, from Tishbe in Gilead, said to Ahab, "As the Lord, the God of Israel, lives, whom I serve, there will be neither dew nor rain in the next few years except at my word" (1 Kings 17:1 NIV).

Elijah was told by God to prophesy no rain, so he said, "No rain until I say again that it will rain." No other prophet had done that until that date, so he was obviously a man anointed of God.

Here is what you have got to look at in the Old Covenant. There was an anointing that came on people for a specific service that they were to perform. They had a touch. You have an indwelling. If they can do that with a touch, what are you called to do? They had a touch, but you have a fullness. Stop limiting yourself.

Then the word of the Lord came to Elijah: "Leave here, turn eastward and hide in the Kerith Ravine, east of the Jordan. You will drink from the brook, and I have directed the ravens to supply you with food there."

> So he did what the Lord had told him. He went to the Kerith Ravine, east of the Jordan, and stayed there. The ravens brought him bread and meat in the morning and bread and meat in the evening, and he drank from the brook (1 Kings 17:2-6 NIV).

From there, the Lord said, "I want you to go to Cherith, by the Brook Cherith, and I want you to camp out there basically until I say otherwise, and I am going to have a raven feed you day and night." What do you think Elijah was thinking at this point? "I am a good Jewish boy! I don't eat carrion bird food." But there was no argument. You see, when you know the voice of God, it doesn't matter what your religious tradition says. You obey God.

So he went and camped by the Brook Cherith, and he drank of the brook, and he ate morning and night. But here is the interesting thing. The name Cherith means circumcision and cutting. So there was a deeper work of sanctification God was doing in his life because he had a destiny. You find this happening all through Scripture. God was changing his character.

> You have got to be careful what you speak or what you allow to come out of your mouth because it shapes your future

Finally the brook dried up, but Elijah had already prophesied his own deliverance. He didn't know it back when he prophesied. He spoke, "No rain until I say it," in obedience to God, and it gave him his own deliverance shortly thereafter. You don't know if what you are speaking today is going to change your tomorrow. You have got to realize that. You have got to be careful what you speak or what you allow to come out of your mouth because it shapes your future.

Zarephath

From there, God told him to dwell at Zarephath.

> *Some time later the brook dried up because there had been no rain in the land. Then the word of the Lord came to him: "Go at once to Zarephath in the region of Sidon and stay there" (1 Kings 17:7-9 NIV).*

The previous place had been a camping, and this one was a dwelling. Zarephath means purifying and refining and a fusing together with. It speaks of the fiery furnace; it speaks of gold that is tried in a furnace that is seven times hotter. It means going from the flesh life to the Spirit life. That's where he is going to live now. Wow! I have got to live in the fiery furnace forever? Yes! Because the Lord is going to perfect your character. From there he said, "Now go up! Now you are ready for My glory. The place of My glory is Mount Carmel." Do you notice that on Mount Carmel the glory wasn't this ooh-and-aah wonderful sensation? This isn't all fun and warm and fuzzy. No, it was confrontational.

We are always crying, "Oh! God! Send Your glory!" You'd better stand back! Ready yourself because the glory is going to deal with your flesh. Flesh cannot stand in the presence of a holy God, so the first thing the glory does is it deals with those issues of the flesh. As a matter of fact, it is even more amazing to me that we are always crying out, "Lord, send me more, we want more glory." You are seated with Christ in heavenly places. You can't get any more than that, and He is in you. So you are in glory and the glory is in you. What are you asking for? How about asking, "Lord, give me the revelation of the glory"? Because it is already in you, and you are already in the glory. In Isaiah 6 it says the whole earth is filled with His glory.

> *And one cried unto another, and said, Holy, holy, holy, is the Lord of hosts: the whole earth is full of his glory (Isaiah 6:3 KJV).*

There is a disconnect somewhere, and it is not with God. It is with our understanding. So the glory is here all the time. You just have to learn how to activate and walk in it, and it comes by agreeing with the revelation of the Word.

And that leads us back to practice. OK. How do I practice? We are going to get there. So then from there Elijah went up to Mount Carmel.

So Obadiah went to meet Ahab and told him, and Ahab went to meet Elijah. When he saw Elijah, he said to him, "Is that you, you troubler of Israel?"

"I have not made trouble for Israel," Elijah replied. "But you and your father's family have. You have abandoned the Lord's commands and have followed the Baals. Now summon the people from all over Israel to meet me on Mount Carmel. And bring the four hundred and fifty prophets of Baal and the four hundred prophets of Asherah, who eat at Jezebel's table."

So Ahab sent word throughout all Israel and assembled the prophets on Mount Carmel. Elijah went before the people and said, "How long will you waver between two opinions?

If the Lord is God, follow him; but if Baal is God, follow him" (1 Kings 18:16-21 NIV).

You know, the hardest work was after the glory, when he had to take off the heads of 850 false prophets—450 of Baal, 400 of Asherah—that's a lot of work! So now he was tired. He was sitting up on the top of Mount Carmel, leaning on his knees, and he told his servant, "I hear the sound of an abundance of rain. Go look."

> *And Elijah said to Ahab, "Go, eat and drink, for there is the sound of a heavy rain." So Ahab went off to eat and drink, but Elijah climbed to the top of Carmel, bent down to the ground and put his face between his knees.*
>
> *"Go and look toward the sea," he told his servant. And he went up and looked.*
>
> *"There is nothing there," he said.*
>
> *Seven times Elijah said, "Go back."*
>
> *The seventh time the servant reported, "A cloud as small as a man's hand is rising from the sea."*
>
> *So Elijah said, "Go and tell Ahab, 'Hitch up your chariot and go down before the rain stops you'" (1 Kings 18:41-44 NIV).*

Seven times he was sent out to look and there was nothing at all there. Finally the servant was going, "Really? Again? OK. I'll keep going." Finally he said, "Well, I am really tired of going up this mountain. I see a cloud about the size of a man's hand," and Elijah says, "Sometimes prophets can seem weird in their revelation." Really? A cloud the size of a man's hand is the abundance of rain? How did you come to that conclusion? He said, "You go tell Ahab to hurry up and get in his chariot and run because the water is going to wash him away."

The next day, Elijah got up and outran the chariot. Not bad for an old guy. The day after that, as he was going wherever he was going, a servant of Jezebel came and told him he had a message for him from Jezebel. The message was, "See if I don't do to you tomorrow about this time what you did to my prophets."

> He saw that message in his imagination, and that became his reality

> Now Ahab told Jezebel everything Elijah had done and how he had killed all the prophets with the sword. So Jezebel sent a messenger to Elijah to say, *"May the gods deal with me, be it ever so severely, if by this time tomorrow I do not make your life like that of one of them"* (1 Kings 19:1-2 NIV).

And the Scripture says when he saw that, he fled. Saw what? The skinny messenger? Elijah had just killed 850 people! The scroll? No. He meditated upon what Jezebel told him and that became his reality. He saw his head coming off. He saw that message in his imagination, and that became his reality and caused him to flee.

Sanctified Imagination

This is a biblical principal. Jesus said if a man looks at a woman and lusts, it is already done.

> *But I tell you that anyone who looks at a woman lustfully has already committed adultery with her in his heart (Matthew 5:28 NIV).*

What you see in your imagination becomes your reality. So we have got to learn to sanctify this thing and bring it into obedience to the Word of God. So when I talk about practice, I mean that I sanctify my imagination and see the reality of this. The reason is that what you focus on you connect with and it becomes your reality. That's how this works. That's Scripture. We can go through many different scriptures that teach the same thing. As a matter of fact, the word imagination is intertwined in this scripture so often that people are shocked by it. You have probably heard it said many times that you can't imagine things, that doing that is of the devil! Most of the time it is because their imagination is unsanctified, but Christian—grow up! Wash your imagination in the blood. Bring it into obedience to the Word of God.

> *Casting down imaginations, and every high thing that exalteth itself against the knowledge of God, and bringing into captivity every thought to the obedience of Christ (2 Corinthians 10:5 KJV).*

Scripture says that you shall meditate upon the Word of God, right? The word for meditate is also translated imagine. In Joshua 1:8 it speaks of imagination. If you will imagine this word day and night, you will be successful.

> *This book of the law shall not depart out of thy mouth; but thou shalt meditate therein day and night, that thou mayest observe to do according to all that is written therein: for then thou shalt make thy way prosperous, and then thou shalt have good success (Joshua 1:8 KJV).*

Why? Because you see it. Abraham had the promise, "as the sand and stars," and that's all he saw.

> *I will surely bless you and make your descendants as numerous as the stars in the sky and as the sand on the seashore. Your descendants will take possession of the cities of their enemies (Genesis 22:17 NIV).*

The sand and stars—they became his reality. You shall love the Lord your God with all your heart, with all your might, with all your strength, and all your mind.

> *He answered, "Love the Lord your God with all your heart and with all your soul and with all your strength and with all your mind'; and, 'Love your neighbor as yourself" (Luke 10:27 NIV).*

That word mind is also imagination. How do you love God with your imagination? You see yourself talking with Him. You see Him. That's how you also develop in your ability to see in the unseen realm. Do you know what? The imagination, the sanctified imagination builds the bridge between the natural and the spiritual, and activation comes in. You can see Him with your eyes wide open, as clear as you see anything. So, arise and shine. How do you shine? You see it. You see it.

What you focus on becomes your reality. There is a brother who has become a friend of ours and is helping to put curriculum together for a school we are developing. His name is Michael Van Vlymen. I highly recommend his books: How to See in the Spirit and Angelic Visitations. But Michael heard the teaching I did on translation by faith on Sid Roth's television program It's Supernatural. He said, "Well, that's easy enough." He is given to this. This is his spiritual DNA. He loves praying and he spends hours every day doing so. Sometimes he will come home from work, eat his meal, spend time with his family, and then he will go to his prayer chair. He prays all night long. But he got this revelation: "Lord, that is in Your Word. I see it is in Your Word. I want to do this." So he would sit in his prayer chair and he would see himself going somewhere in the world to minister. He said, "You know, Lord, I know this is me, but I am practicing. Lord, just so You know, I am ready any time You want."

He kept practicing it, and within three months he started going. You're thinking, "I wish I could do that!" Well, I wish you would too, because I know you can.

6

LET THERE BE LIGHT

Simple Steps of Faith

This is not rocket science, and sometimes that is the problem. Most people want rocket science. I can't even understand that. Forget about rocket science and take some simple steps of faith. Arise and shine for your light—not His light—your light has come. There is the identifier. You are in Him, you are His body, and you carry a residue or a facet of His light that He has given to you. Arise, shine, for your light has come. Wait a minute—has come. There are some Hebraic studies that say it is not "has come" but your light has now come to realization. It has always been yours, but now there is a realization, a revelation of "Hey! This is who I am." Arise! Shine! For your light has now come and the glory of the Lord is risen upon you!

You see, when you get the revelation that you are light, all of a sudden His glory begins to rise upon you. Why? Let me put it this way. Scripture says God is light and in Him is no darkness at all, right? Well, let's change the word light.

God is love and in Him is no darkness at all. Any facet of the character of Jesus fits into the word light because that is His character. God is glory and in Him is no darkness at all because that is His character. God is wisdom and in

Him is no ignorance. Do you understand? So light encompasses all that He is and all the facets of His character are in this light that you are. Now, through the process of agreeing with who we are we begin to operate in what He is—light. So, arise! Shine! For your light has come.

In other words, this light is His character, and His character is what He says you need to be. You can't separate this, but we have to understand it if we want to walk in this realm of glory that has come upon the earth right now. This last dispensation, this last great move of God—it is beginning this year. It is already starting. There are things beginning to happen around the earth. We have heard bits and pieces; I am telling you to get ready, because here it comes.

> Any facet of the character of Jesus fits into the word light because that is His character

> *For, behold, the darkness shall cover the earth, and gross darkness the people: but the Lord shall arise upon thee, and his glory shall be seen upon thee (Isaiah 60:2 KJV).*

That speaks of the end of the age. But—however—the Lord will arise over you. Wait a minute. You are light. You are coming to that realization. His glory is going to arise on you, and He is going to cover you. He is going to arise over you.

We think some people are just anointed, but what does it mean when we see the glory upon them? Consider Mark

9 and the Mount of Transfiguration. The Lord began to glow. That glory that was resident within Him began to radiate from within, and it changed everything about Him so that they said that His clothes were so clean and bright no launderer on earth could have managed it. They began to see a transformation, and as this transformation took place the veil between two realms was open and He was talking with Moses and Elijah face to face.

> *After six days Jesus took Peter, James and John with him and led them up a high mountain, where they were all alone. There he was transfigured before them. His clothes became dazzling white, whiter than anyone in the world could bleach them. And there appeared before them Elijah and Moses, who were talking with Jesus (Mark 9:2-4 NIV).*

Here is the interesting thing about this: Isaiah 46:10 says that God declares the end from the beginning.

> *Declaring the end from the beginning, and from ancient times the things that are not yet done, saying, "My counsel shall stand, and I will do all my pleasure" (Isaiah 46:10).*

If you want to understand the end of the age, you need to understand the beginning. In the beginning God said, "Let there be light." At the end we also see light. When God said, "Let there be light," He spoke and 186,300 miles per second sprang forth. A big bang, if you will—instant light. So all of this natural realm is a created light that you have authority over. Scientists have theorized (especially Einstein) that as you approach the speed of light, time slows down. You have heard, I am sure, that if you send somebody at almost the speed of light to Mars and back, it will take them two hours, but back on Earth 50 years will have elapsed. So time slows down, but when you hit the speed of light, time stops. You step back into eternity.

Light is actually electromagnetic radiation emanating from a source, and it extends in a color spectrum from red to violet. It goes on forever. Light, when it is released, continues on. That's why you see stars in the skies, though some of them burnt out billions of light years ago; we are still seeing them now because light continues. What you speak also continues, and it either sheds light or darkness. So electromagnetic radiation, light, and God exist outside of the realm of time.

Antwerp, Middle Ages

Let me share with you a story. I didn't share this for a long time because I had no paradigm for it. At the time it was something totally outside my grid, so to speak. I was in my study praying one day and minding my own business when all of a sudden I was literally moved by the Spirit of God, and I found myself in Antwerp, in the Middle Ages. It was pouring down rain; the streets were muddy and hard to traverse due to the mud. A wagon came slogging through this muck, and there was a little boy sitting there in the mud weeping. I went over to him, and I said, "What is the matter?"

He said, "My mommy is dying and they won't let me in to see her." I asked why. "There is a plague," he replied.

I said, "Take me to her." And in his face I saw a little spark of hope. He grabbed my hand and he led me through the squalor to a home, and we opened the door. There was a bed in the middle of the floor. A man was sitting there, the woman's husband, and someone else off in the corner, but I had no immediate revelation of who he was. I think it was an angel.

> I was literally moved by the Spirit of God, and I found myself in Antwerp, in the Middle Ages

The man cried out, "No! Don't come in! Plague!" I said it was OK. I entered the house and stood at the foot of the bed, and I looked at this woman. She was aware. I began to preach the Gospel to them. Then I asked if they would like to accept Jesus, and they all said yes! So this family accepted the Lord as their Savior, and then I prayed for the woman's healing, and she came out of the bed totally healed! And then I was back in my office.

The whole experience was a huge learning curve. "What was that, Lord?" I asked Him.

The Lord said, "Google it."

So I went over to my computer and typed in plague, Antwerp, and Middle Ages. The results showed that the bubonic plague started in the Jewish Quarter in Antwerp; it killed thousands of people and they evicted the Jews because they blamed them for the plague. I told the Lord, "I will never share this! Nobody would ever believe this. I don't even understand this myself. How can I have traveled back in history?"

He said, "Don't limit Me. Before the foundation of the world, written into the curriculum of history was this encounter that I brought you back to affect. You have just reached the point in your life when this encounter was enacted, but they had it way back then." And I didn't really understand, so He said, "Keep studying light."

You see, light is eternal. It is past, present, and future all at the same time. God is light. John experienced this on the Isle of Patmos. God called John up, and he was flown to the end of the age and wrote down what he saw. I continued studying light as God commanded, but I still did not want to share it.

Light is eternal. It is past, present, and future all at the same time

I felt that way until I talked with a friend who said, "Yes, that has also happened to me, but I have never shared it." I jokingly told him I couldn't imagine why!

But it is all there in the study of light. We are speaking of created light, mind you. The light of God, who is light Himself, is a higher order. This is the light that we are created out of, so He has authority over us. Creative light over created light, in essence. I know that this gets a little challenging. But God will give you the revelation. It sometimes challenges me as well, and I am still working through it. Do you know life cannot exist without light?

The end result of life without light is nothing, and God is light. If you don't have Him, you have nothing.

You can't measure darkness. You cannot contain it, and you can't take it into a laboratory or test it in any way, but you can do all this with light. For a number of years I was teaching about this, thinking, "I am going to get a Nobel Prize in Science someday" because I had made a discovery. I found something faster than the speed of light—darkness. Think about it. When light comes, what happens to darkness? It is gone, right? And people I shared this with would all have a good laugh at me. Three years later, Reshma's best friend was at home watching the Discovery Channel, and she watched a program declaring that they just discovered darkness is faster than light. It turns out I just didn't write my paper quick enough!

Now, think about this for a moment—you are light. When you step into the room, the devil's reaction is, "Shhh! It's a Christian!" He's afraid! But Christians have always acted like, "The devil is here! Shhh!" The devil is terrified of you if you know who you are in Christ! You are light and he is darkness, and light dispels darkness. So when you just walk into a place, he flees! Start living in the revelation of that! It is fun!

Light Dispels Darkness

We were in Ireland talking with some friends before I really understood fully what this was all about. I was explaining to them how light dispels darkness as we left our meeting. I said, "Don't be surprised when you are walking down the street and demons just start to manifest because of the light you carry."

They figured I was full of blarney. But then a guy walked past us into a phone booth. From the phone booth he turned around toward us, and he looked like Marilyn Manson; he was just completely demonized, and in a totally demonic voice he said, "Go home!"

My friends jumped and said, "What was that?" I told them it was just a demon.

What did I do? I didn't do anything because God didn't tell me to. I did ask Him, but I am not going to jump into a fight without knowing I am going to win. You do what the Father tells you to do. Our friends went, "Wow!" Reshma and I smiled at each other and watched them out of the corner of our eye. They were looking at each other the way a husband and wife sometimes communicate. We walked a little further and there were two young ladies nearby. We were in a university district, and these girls were standing there talking a short distance away from us. All of a sudden they let out this blood-curdling scream in the middle of the thoroughfare! Our friends jumped from surprise—I can still see it. They said, "Dear God, what was that?" I told them it was demons—get used to this. By then they believed it. You see, if you understand you are light, this is normal to you. You don't have to worry about being in crowds anymore. It makes your Christian life a little more exciting and fun.

It is interesting that light is one of the major features of near-death experiences. I don't know why they call them near-death experiences. To me it is near-life. Someone dies—they are gone and cold, sometimes for many hours, and yet they call it "near-death." I have had a fascination with this from the 1970s when I worked at TBN (Trinity Broadcasting Network) and I met Dr. Richard Eby and Betty Maltz and all of these other people who have had these "I'm dead" experiences. It seems that every one of them sees a light in these experiences. Why do they see a light? Because God is light.

Here is another fascinating thing about light. Light exhibits an uncanny awareness—an unexplained awareness. Light has a consciousness. Have you ever heard of the double-split experiment in physics? They take a wave of light and they split it, but then it comes back together. That is an "impossible" thing, yet it happens.

The wave of light can split, travel great distances across the galaxy, and then still come back together. That awareness occurs instantly; hence, it is faster than the speed of light. Think of this in terms of creation, remembering that God is light and we are created light—split off from the original Source of all light.

Here is another fascinating truth—scientists have also found out that beams of light are helical. What does that mean? The helix is a three-dimensional shape like a corkscrew or spiral staircase. Human DNA is a helix. The orbital angular momentum of light is a helix and you can see it. Don't ask me how, but they have discovered this, and they are mystified.

> *In the beginning God created the heaven and the earth (Genesis 1:1 KJV).*

If you read that in the Hebrew, in the beginning God created "et" the heavens and the earth. There is a connector word "et" in Hebrew that is never translated into English. And it is used over 9,820 times in Scripture. "Et" is spelled with two Hebrew letters—aleph and tav. You may be more familiar with the Greek equivalents—Alpha and Omega. Aleph Tav is the A to Z of the Hebrew alphabet.

Now, the aleph is believed to have come from an ancient hieroglyph for the number one; it also symbolizes a strong leader. Tav comes from the mark of a cross and symbolizes covenant. So including all the Hebrew word pictures, we read: "In the beginning, God created the message of the first strong leader who will come in the sign of the cross." There are many, many such examples. This is a picture in the Scriptures that God created the Hebrew alphabet in the beginning, and that was the helix that held everything together—the Word of His power.

The Building Blocks of Creation

Many of you probably know of Dr. David Van Koevering, the quantum physicist. He is a friend of ours. One day his good friend on the human genome project, a study of human DNA, called him and said, "You have got to come down here. We have a problem here and we don't know what to do." He asked what it was and they responded, "Just come down." So he went down to the lab and he had to clear all the security protocols and things of that nature to even get into the lab. Everything they do there, they video tape or record. So he arrived and asked what the problem was. They said, "Look at this!" And they played the video for him to look at and said, "Please explain this to us."

Dr. Van Koevering was looking at the video and said, "Explain what?" They told him that every strand of human DNA has the ancient Hebrew alphabet imprinted upon it. "How could that be?" He responded, "I don't know."

> You have the ancient Hebrew alphabet embedded in your human DNA

Dr. Van Koevering was sitting with us at lunch one day after a meeting at Gateway in Coeur D Alene, Idaho and he was telling us this incredible story regarding the DNA. He made it clear that he still did not fully understand why each strand of human DNA had the ancient Hebrew alphabet encoded in it.

Reshma said, "Well, that's simple. In the beginning God created the heavens and the earth. In the book of John chapter one verse one it states, *"In the beginning was the Word, and the Word was with God, and the Word was God."*

And in John 1:14 it says, *"And the Word was made flesh, and dwelt among us..."*

That's it! You have the ancient Hebrew alphabet embedded in your human DNA. It is the same particle of light. You are light!

Light travels from its source and immediately reflects off of every object that it comes in contact with. I like that because God is light, and we are supposed to reflect that light, as seen in Isaiah 60:1. Arise! Shine! Your light has come, and the glory of the Lord has risen upon you. His light will arise upon you. So our light reflects His light. When I have taught about this (as God allows me to), people have taken photographs during the services, and they have looked at the photographs later and said, "In the photo you are nothing but a ball of light up there." That is a confirmation! This is not about look at me! It has got nothing to do with me—it is the Word, and God confirms His Word.

We were recently in the Philippines in front of ten thousand people and 42 different provinces by satellite, and they all saw the same thing—light. I told the Lord that was a good confirmation! That's just one reason why I know this is reality. This is a year of Isaiah 60.

This is a progression that is coming to fruition by the end of this year—people are going to see the light of God's glory on you. They are going to see it with wide-open eyes. At this point it is only cameras catching it, but they are going to see this, and when they see the light of the glory of God risen upon you, they are going to be drawn to that. "Dude, what is that?" They are going to be compelled. Look out, Charles Finney! Look and see! This is what God is releasing.

Light is only the visible frequency of the electromagnetic spectrum. Other forms of radiation are radio waves, microwaves, infrared, visible white light, ultraviolet light, etc. Light is also emitted from a source of heat. Our God is a Consuming Fire, so you can say you are a "hunka

hunka burning love." Alright! Heat and light are almost always simultaneous.

To recap, the Lord created us in the same way that He manifested light. Light travels in helical waves; in other words, light travels in the same way that DNA wraps itself in a double helix. God created the very fabric of our being to work in tandem with His light.

Now, again, back to Isaiah 46—God declares the end from the beginning.

> *Declaring the end from the beginning, and from ancient times things that are not yet done, saying, "My counsel shall stand, and I will do all My pleasure" (Isaiah 46:10).*

Clothed in Light

In the beginning Adam and Eve walked and talked with God face to face every day. After the fall, they realized they were naked—the moment they ate of the tree of the knowledge of good and evil. Prior to that, they were clothed in light as a garment—just as our God is clothed in light as a garment. It was the glory that covered them! Their spirit man was in the preeminent position, so they were clothed in light, and they didn't recognize physical nakedness because they couldn't see it. They were clothed in light because the natural man took the proper position of submission to the spirit man. But when they fell into sin, when they ate of the tree of knowledge, their spirit did not manifest the light that had previously covered them and they were naked. God is calling us back to light, and we are going to be clothed in that light.

That is why people are going to see us and see the light of the glory of God, and they are going to come running to that, because within every human being is a recognition in their spirit. There is a knowing that there is a reality that we haven't connected with, and when they see the reality their spirit is going to know it and be drawn to that light like moths to a flame. It is the extravagant love of God that started this process through covenant. He is bringing us full circle back to this same place of intimacy through covenant of the Bride and Groom. It is the whole process.

He declares the end from the beginning. So in the new age when the thousand-year reign comes this will happen? No, there are going to be forerunners who usher in the truth and the reality of the possibilities of God. We are seeing it begin now, and it will carry us through into the Millennial Age. There is a reality that is ours that God has been crying out for us to hear and engage, and it belongs to us now. There is a generation that is alive right now and that is you. I am not talking about strictly the younger generation. If you are alive, you are the generation. We have got to stop separating based upon chronological age. That is ridiculous.

There is a generation that is going to understand what it means to go back and forth between the realm of eternity and this natural realm on a regular basis, because this is normal. That's what Adam and Eve did back then and it was normal. Rabbis have studied the Hebrew and declared that the Garden of Eden was a place outside of time. It was an eternal realm where God said, "With the wisdom I have given you and the revelation that flows through you, you look at their character, and you give them a name that fits their character, or you speak that character into them." So Adam spoke character into every animal, and they were released out of the Garden of Eden into the earth.

This was why the cherubim were placed with a sword to stand guard over the Garden. You can't come back here! There is too much power, there is too much life, and if you eat of the Tree of Life, you will be in this fallen condition for eternity. It is a realm of the spirit, and when Jesus died He said, "You can come back."

The veil in the Temple was 30 feet wide, 60 feet tall, and 18 inches thick, and it had embroidered cherubim on the front with a flaming sword—and it was torn in two at Jesus' death! Your heavenly Father tore that and said, "Come on back, kids; I have missed you." You have access into the Paradise of God because He created it for us. It is an awesome place. By the way, when you travel at the speed of light and you reach the speed of light, at that point you will never age again.

Arise and shine, for your light has come. I am sure you have heard this floating around Christendom for the last few years, but we are going to get a revelation that we never have to age again. It is because of light. When you understand who you truly are, something will shift. I'll let you chew on that one. As a matter of fact, let me say this—Jesus is light and God is light and we are seated with Him in heavenly places. He is in us. So we can say that we are in light and light is in us and the whole earth is filled with light. We just have to learn how to walk in that and engage it. Light is life, and there is no darkness. So if you get a revelation that you are light, there is no more sickness, disease—none of this stuff can affect you anymore because your spirit man takes the preeminent position, and your mortality, your physical body, is clothed with glory. That doesn't make you eternal—not the physical at least. But you are an eternal being. You don't want to keep this raggedy old flesh anyway right? It can be changed to the point where it doesn't decay, it is not defective, and it walks in the intended purposes of God.

> When you understand who you truly are, something will shift

The Light and the Glory

The light manifested in your physical body supersedes decay and death. I get pain in my body sometimes because I injured my back in the Army. For me to stand up and minister for hours used to be agony. I just kept saying, "I release the light there. I release the glory there." What happened? The pain left!

I have done the same thing with my teeth. I had four bad teeth and it was extremely painful! The doctor wanted $17,000 to take care of them, and I told him he was not retiring on my nickel—forget that! So for two weeks I was contending over this and finally I was exhausted. That kind of pain wears you out. I asked the Father, "Father, what are

You saying?" That is my normal language with Him. "What are You saying? I know You are communicating something in this to me."

He said, "Release the glory."

I didn't even say it out loud. Within my heart I just said, "I release the glory," and I had a picture of my teeth in my spirit, and guess what happened? The pain disappeared! Gone! Instantly healed!

I know this is fact because I walk in this. Reshma walks in this. It is not rocket science; it is the reality of the Word. It comes by revelation, but even though I had revelation of this, I didn't immediately exercise my faith. I just kept pleading and begging God, until He said, "Look! I have already put it in you, just do something. Release it." Hallelujah!

It has been fun to watch young kids get this revelation. A young teenage girl heard this, and she and her mother were in the kitchen working, and all of a sudden the dishwasher broke. The mother said, "Oh no! I have got to call the repair man."

But the daughter said, "No! Don't you remember what the minister said?" She put her hands on that dishwasher, and she said, "I release the glory of God!" Death, decay, and corruption don't work in the glory, and that dishwasher started right up and works to this day. I wrote about that in one of our books, but she put it into action—simple faith!

An old farmer heard that testimony and it inspired him to exercise his faith. He had a tractor that was sitting on blocks in his barn for six years. He hadn't done a thing with it, but he thought about this testimony. He put his hands on the tractor and released the glory. Then he started it up, and it was like brand new and has been working ever since.

Revelations of Light

Astrophysicist John Gribbon theorized that an electromagnetic wave (that's light) is everywhere along its path at once, everywhere in the universe, omnipresent. It is everywhere at once. That sounds familiar doesn't it? Or you can also say that distance does not exist for an electromagnetic wave, which is light. Or stated another way, everything in the universe—past, present, and future—is connected to everything else by a web of electromagnetic radiation that sees everything at once. So, in thinking of translocation, how hard is it really? You're light. You are already there. I am not saying you are omnipotent or omnipresent because you are not, but you are in Him, and He is already there. And because you are light, there is no distance. There is no distance. You are the key. You are the key. You are the key. Just agree with it!

7

THE END FROM THE BEGINNING

I am going to explain this revelation a litter further, because as people begin to receive and learn about all this, the Lord has shown me that some can begin to have a great fear of the future. Many things that happen in life and many things that come our way through the world can bring fear to our hearts.

Some believers live in real fear, and some don't really believe that Christ is coming for them. It is the strangest thing. There are people like that because there are so many different views out there that can confuse a believer in so many ways. If you are that person, you know it in your heart. God's word to you is that He is there to bring a breakthrough for you. He wants to touch you and set you free from that.

I want to encourage you that God is in your future. People in your life may have spoken already for you and told you what your destiny is. They have already decided that this is what you are going to be. Sometimes when we are raised in a certain way, there are certain things spoken over us, and we tend to believe them and those lies get settled in our hearts. It is important to know what God's Word says, and it sometimes takes a lot of years to undo some of the lies. There are so many voices speaking, but there are some fundamental basic truths of the Gospel that should be settled in our hearts about God and who He is.

One of those truths is that He died; first, He was born through a virgin, He walked among us, and then He died, He rose again, and He said He is coming back. I am waiting for Him to come back because I am going to see Him. I don't know how the end is going to pan out. Nobody really knows. But the truth is He came in a physical form, He was born, and He walked among us as a 100 percent human being and God in a physical form. He said He would rise again, and then when He rose up a lot of people saw Him. He said He is coming back! He is coming back in a physical form, not a state of mind. That's the truth of the Gospel and that's our blessed hope. I just want to submit that to you. Confusion can come and I know that there are people who are confused, but God wants to set you free.

He is coming for us. He has not forgotten us

He is coming for us. He has not forgotten us. Because there are unbiblical views out there that are contrary to the Gospel, it causes some confusion. Many believe He is not returning for us. It almost sounds like this view is saying that God has kind of forgotten about us. No, He has not. He is coming for you. You have hope in Him. There is a blessed hope. There are a few things that need to be settled in our hearts, and I might step on some toes, but it is alright.

The Revelation of Marriage

We are learning to dance, so let's dance together. One of the things that really is shocking to me is that Christians are even confused about marriage. There are some truths, some fundamental basic truths that need to be settled in our hearts. If it is not settled in our hearts in this hour, we are going to be in a world of hurt, and we do not want to be found wanting in His eyes. And we do not want to be deceived. That is my greatest prayer every day of my life. "Lord God, I do not want to be deceived." So I just want to encourage you that if you have a fear of the future, or if you have a fear today because of the things in your life or the views you have held, and you think that Jesus is not coming back for you, I am here to submit to you that He is. I know this because He is speaking today.

A Prayer

So let's just set this book aside for a moment and do something. Let's close our eyes and let's judge our hearts. God wants to bring a breakthrough, and He is breaking that fear off of us because God has not given us a spirit of fear but of power, love, and a sound mind. He has already defeated the enemy.

Father, we thank You right now in Jesus' name. Lord, I take authority over the spirit of fear that has tried to come upon Your children, Your people, and Lord, I break its power right now in the name of Jesus, and I speak freedom, and liberty, and joy in Jesus' name. And Father,

I pray for confidence to come in Your people now, Lord God, that You are for them, that You are coming for them, that there is a Heaven, that we are ruling and reigning with You, God. And we thank You, Lord Jesus, for Your mercy and for Your love, and this truth being settled in Your people today. And we thank You for it, Father. We thank You, Lord, for Your love, for Your mercy, and for Your grace, for Your understanding, Lord, that You give us. I pray that You will open our hearts to receive Your Word now. Open our ears to hear at a greater level and eyes to see. And we thank You, Lord.

Just take a minute now and receive. We have prayed in faith, now receive. Thank You, Lord. Thank You, Jesus. We praise You, Lord. We love You, Lord. We thank You for Your love in Jesus' name. Thank You, Lord.

The Glowing Ones

We have been talking about light and the revelation the Lord has given me on this subject and how the Lord told me at the beginning of the year this is the year of Isaiah 60 coming to pass in the Body of Christ. Arise and shine, for your light is come and the glory of the Lord is risen upon you. There will be a progression throughout the year, and by the end of the year we are going to be living beacons that will be seen by the world as those who carry the glory of God. I have heard in the spirit, "They will say the glowing ones." That is what the Lord said to me, and I just received it. Then we taught this. There have been a few places that the Lord has released us to teach this revelation. We have had some unusual pictures taken of us during the teaching of this revelation in the Philippines. There were pictures that showed glowing beings on the stage as we taught. It was God confirming His word. Somebody else heard the message and has been teaching it as well, and she sent me a picture of herself teaching. In the picture, she is standing there and she just looks like a being of light. These things are already happening, and they are going to increase.

How do we get from point A to point B? We take a step of faith. I shared that previously, but that is it! It's fascinating to me that God is confirming His Word so quickly now. Only a few years ago it seemed to take a while, and then we would see a confirmation. An apostle we know was telling us that he saw a confirmation to the words he spoke sometimes 10, 15, or 20 years later! Things are happening much quicker now. There is an acceleration of time. One thing that Reshma reminded me of was Isaiah 46:10:

> *Declaring the end from the beginning, and from ancient times the things that are not yet done, saying, My counsel shall stand, and I will do all my pleasure (Isaiah 46:10 KJV).*

We look back at Genesis to understand Revelation. We always look back to the beginning to understand fully anything in Scripture. The beginning of the Church is not what it is going to look like at the end. The beginning was seed form. What does maturity look like? The early church was a starting point, so what does the finished work look like? I can tell you it's not a raggedy bunch of people dragging along and trying to cross the finish line, but rather a glorious Church! He said the glory of the later house shall outshine the former. So we look at the beginning to understand the end.

First Mention

In theological studies, they call this the principle of first mention. It is scriptural. But there is some understanding that needs to come. Let me share an example. When Adam was put into a deep sleep and God took the rib closest to his heart and created his wife, Eve, do you know what he said? He said, "This is bone of my bone and flesh of my flesh." What is the common expression? This is my flesh and blood. Do you remember doubting Thomas? Everybody singles out Thomas and I don't know why. Every one of them doubted until they saw. So Thomas wasn't the bad guy, he was just the last guy to have the proof. But still Jesus said to him, "Put your finger in the hole in my hand," telling him He was flesh and bone. Adam and Eve were flesh and bone. Jesus, when He rose from the dead, was flesh and bone. We are talking about resurrected bodily life. That's an applied example of first mention.

> What does maturity look like? The early church was a starting point

> *Who coverest thyself with light as with a garment: who stretchest out the heavens like a curtain (Psalms 104:2 KJV).*

Doctors have identified and discovered that blood is congealed light. It is that which was perfect that fell into darkness because of the tree of the knowledge of good and evil. So the light congealed and became what we know as blood. But we can come back to what was in the beginning with Adam and Eve, as now Jesus has brought us back through His blood and redeemed us. Now He is flesh and bone, and His blood is the light that is life for us. In the natural realm, the life is in the blood, even in Christ, because He shed His blood and life is in that blood. But now we are light, and light and life are the same thing.

What God is revealing now at this hour is not something that has never been revealed before. We are going back to the beginning to understand who we truly are and what He is trying to bring us into in this hour. It is an hour of Daniel. In the Book of Daniel, he was told:

> *But thou, O Daniel, shut up the words, and seal the book, even to the time of the end: many shall run to and fro, and knowledge shall be increased (Daniel 12:4 KJV).*

That is a prophetic word and not just about Daniel but about much of Scripture. There are times and seasons. You've heard that there are times and seasons for everything under the sun.

> *To every thing there is a season, and a time to every purpose under the heaven (Ecclesiastes 3:1 KJV).*

This is the time and the season when great revelation and unveiling of the hidden things and mysteries of the Kingdom is being released in this generation. There has never been a greater time to be alive and to be a follower of Jesus and a disciple of God, because He is investing Himself in you in a way that has never been done before. If we just grab hold of this, we can feast on revelation every day.

Consider this scripture:

> *But, beloved, be not ignorant of this one thing, that one day is with the Lord as a thousand years, and a thousand years as one day (2 Peter 3:8 KJV).*

The Morning of the Third Day

From the time of Jesus until the turn of the century we have completed 2,000 years or two days. Now we are early in the morning on the third day. From the time of Adam until the turn of the century, we have completed 6,000 years, or six days, and now we are early in the morning on the seventh day. This is basic prophetic understanding. As a matter of fact, the rabbis, when they began to figure out the sequence of time from the beginning of Adam said it was June of 2015 that ended the 6,000th year and began the 7,000th year. We have just crossed into this fullness-of-time season.

It is now just prior to the manifestation of the return of Messiah for all mankind, and there is going to be glory for those who are following God and judgment for those who are not. So here we are. It is on the seventh day—the Sabbath, or Shabbat. It was the custom of Jesus to visit the Temple. You are the Temple. On this seventh day, it is His custom to visit you, the Temple, so you can expect visitation every day.

This is Scripture and it is not a stretch. Visitation happens all the time. Twenty years ago it may have been rare, but now so many people are understanding this and walking in the reality of visitation from the Lord. It is the seventh day and God is going to do a quick work because we don't have 30, 50, or 80 years to walk out this process of character development. On the seventh day when He visits the temple He will do a quick work. Remember the woman who was bent over for 18 years and couldn't lift herself up? It was on a Sabbath day that Jesus visited this temple, and He saw this woman in this condition. That spoke of the inward man. You have got to see this through a prophetic lens. You are the temple. You are the priest of the temple. You can minister the Word of God in your own temple every day. That's why you spend time in the Word. So here she was, bent over, and there was Jesus. She was not praying, she was not begging for release, she was not interceding. Jesus saw her condition. Nobody asked Him anything, He just saw the need and He said, "You're loosed." He laid His hands on her and instantly she became whole. That's what visitation does. It takes you from your snail pace to a quantum leap. It releases you from bondages and sets you free to follow Him. That's visitation. That's why this hour is so extraordinary. So many people are having visitations.

> We have just crossed into this fullness-of-time season

Whosoever Will

Have you heard about the preacher children in Brazil? Little children are coming under a heavy anointing and mantle of God and are going out on the streets and witnessing, winning people to Jesus, starting churches, and pastoring them. They have hundreds of people in their congregations, and when they preach it is the wisdom of God that flows from them. The Spirit of God in the children is not any smaller than the Spirit of God in you. As a matter of fact, He is less hindered in children. That is why He told us to come as little children (see Matt. 18:3).

There has never been a day like this. This visitation is happening in Indonesia, Brazil, the Middle East, and in many different parts of the world. What a glorious day! But this is not just about the young generation. It is the fulfillment of Scripture, and it is to anybody who will. It is an hour of visitation. That's why God is going to do in a moment what takes a lifetime. So how do we position ourselves?

We say, "Father, I am listening. I have been waiting for You," and He shows up. Adam and Eve were flesh and bone, and Jesus is flesh and bone, and when they ate of the tree of the knowledge of good and evil light was congealed into blood. But the new creation and what we are moving toward is back to light. You can meditate on that for a while. So we move at the speed of light, where time slows down. The distance to another location simply folds in upon itself, and we can get there instantly. That is what we call translocation. This is what God has been teaching me, and that is why it is so exciting—because He said this is the year! Are you getting this? This is the year that His light is coming. Arise and shine, your light has come and His glory is risen upon you!

Released into the Supernatural

This is the year of translocation! This is the year of being released into this realm of supernatural ministry! Years ago, back in the early 2000s, when I was first learning this and praying into it, I said, "Lord, I am ready for my first lesson." I was in a car on the beach in Seattle, Washington and was going all the way back to Spokane, Washington. That trip takes about five and a half to six hours, depending on traffic and the time of day. So my friend John and I laid hands on the car. This car was old and raggedy, with baling wire and chewing gum holding it together, and maybe a few pieces of duct tape. Remember the Flintstones? That's what this was—a Flintstone car. So we laid hands on the dashboard and prayed, my friend and I, and we put his CD in the CD player and played just one song, "This Is the Air I Breathe." And we just started driving. Now, I was expecting a lesson, you know? Preconceived, perhaps in my mind. "Lord, here is how You are supposed to do this." I remember every turn through the Snoqualmie Pass; we came down the pass, pulled off into Vantage, we stopped for lunch and filled up with gas, and we got back on the road. I remember we did the whole trip just singing that one song. That trip took less than two hours! I asked the Lord, "What was that?" We were both thinking, "Now, wait a minute. We were expecting a lesson, Lord, but that's not funny! What just happened, Lord?" This is what He told me way back then.

The Lord said that we had learned in school that the shortest distance between two points is a straight line. We move through time that way too—in a straight line, always moving forward. God said He had folded time. The Lord said, "Actually, the shortest distance is already being there."

I never fully comprehended that, and that's when I started studying physics. I never understood it until He said to study light. That's what this is. Remember the key? You are the same frequency as that key made of light, and you are the key. You're in Christ. He is omnipresent. He is everywhere. It is not a stretch to go from here to anywhere around the world because He is already there and you are in Him, and you are there. Boom! You just agree with that. Welcome to the outer limits. This isn't even the beginning. Do you have to go faster than the speed of light to go from this planet way out into the third heaven? No you don't, because the third heaven is not way out there, it is all around us. It all fits in the span of His hand, so where He is, it is the third heaven. As a matter of fact, the Kingdom of Heaven is within you!

Actually, the shortest distance is already being there

We always think about the third heaven as being way out there. But it is so close, it is right where you are. Don't make things so far away and so difficult to attain because it is all already here right now. Just agree with God. You are a being of light. It is so fun to watch this as people get it and the light comes on. I told you light is also energy. God is light, so He must have an inexhaustible, immeasurable amount of energy, power, and might. Here is provision from Heaven—He has given into you and invested in you all power to overcome anything.

> *You made them rulers over the works of your hands; you put everything under their feet (Psalms 8:6 NIV).*

Ascending into Heavenly Realms

One time when I was caught up into the third heaven, I was visiting with my aunt who had graduated to Heaven a couple of years earlier. Behind her there was this very tall angel, and he had what looked like a Torah scroll. But he kept looking at me, and after I was done speaking with my aunt, I said, "Excuse me, who are you?"

He said, "I am the angel of provision that God has assigned to release the provisioning of Heaven for all of His saints at the end of the age." That which at first looked like a Torah scroll was actually a manifest. It had every provision categorized and listed. He said, "I will be seeing you again."

Later, when we were ministering in Kuala Lumpur, Malaysia, the church we were speaking at was in the middle of a building program. They were in the process of building this brand new facility which would be four stories tall.

The architectural plans were beautiful and we were excited

with them and for them. In the meantime, the church continued meeting in their leased space which was very small. We always loved going there as this place was like Heaven on earth! Some of the most amazing miracles we have ever seen, we saw in this church. While I was ministering, along came this angel of provision. He was just standing there in the church looking at me, when suddenly the spirit of prophecy came upon me, so I began to prophesy about the provisioning of heaven for what God has called them to build.

The fun part is that they took a picture during the service, and they actually caught the scroll in the picture. You can see that picture on our website. After the service the pastor said, "Would you come out to the building site? We want you to see it." They were excited, and we were excited, and it was an awesome time.

So we went down there, and the pastor said, "We have only got enough rebar and steel to build the foundation and the footing. Would you pray together with us that God will bring millionaires along to bless this project financially? We only have a short time to do this, and we need somewhere between seven and nine million dollars."

So I asked the Father, "Father, how do we pray?"

And He said, "Don't pray for money. Pray over the cement and rebar, that I will multiply the materials." In obedience we prayed over the cement and rebar and they were able to build the whole building as the materials kept multiplying until the project was completed. That is supernatural provision!

Supernatural Increase

There is a seed time and harvest that is natural. Don't ever neglect that, but expect supernatural provision. That's why you can't dictate things to God. "God, I gave You this, now You give me that." No—you say, "Lord, I give because I love You and You give because You know my need better than I do, and so I am not going to tell you how to do that." That was a radical change for us. Something else I want to share is that you should expect the unexpected. How do you do that? Just expect God to do what God does. He loves to surprise us. That's what we have heard, and that's what we know. He is the greatest giver that you will ever know. As a matter of fact, when it comes to believing God, I am going to jump in with both feet! You can call me crazy if you want to; I don't care. The Lord has allowed me to visit many heavenly places.

when it comes to believing God, I am going to jump in with both feet

Once while in worship, I was having an open vision, and in this vision I went to the River of Life and He gave me a knapsack. At the bottom the river were all of these beautiful gemstones that we talk about, and the Lord said, "Grab a handful," so I did, and put them in the knapsack. He then took me into Paradise, the Garden, and He said, "Take some food off the tree and put it in the knapsack." Then He took me back to the library in Heaven. I had been there before and there is a desk there with some scrolls located behind it. He said, "Grab some scrolls and put them in your knapsack." I did, and then He said, "Leave the knapsack just inside the portal, the doorway that you access, because you are going to hand all this stuff out."

Here is a promise that God has given us and not because I was looking for this. We do prophetic gestures and it looks foolish, but I don't care because lives have been changed and I praise God for it. But a man who is great in my estimation and is a solid prophet of God said the day is coming when we are going to reach into that realm and bring tangibly back those things God is showing us in the Spirit, and we are going to be handing them to people.

I said, "God, I'm in." So when He said this to me, I said, "Lord, You know I am expecting this. I am expecting tangible manifestation. People are going to get their healing because they are going to eat the fruit." I was getting excited.

In the next chapter we'll look at Isaiah 60 a little bit more. In Isaiah 60:1 it says to arise and shine. Now we'll look down to verse 8 for an application of light.

Endnotes

1. Dr. Rogers W.B., Blood Alchemy (n.d.) (The Metaphysics and Science of The Blood of Christ)
2. Shaw G., (n.d.) The End-times Handmaidens and Servants
3. Copeland K. (n.d.) The Day the Glory Invaded Hell

8

THOSE WHO GLOW

Who are these that fly as a cloud, and as the doves to their windows? (Isaiah 60:8 KJV)

My first inclination toward the supernatural of God—as a child of four years old—was as a perceiver. I had to learn to be a seer. I wasn't born a seer. During my journey, I learned that I have spiritual senses and that I can exercise them so that I become proficient in the usage of them. It is very similar to how we develop in the natural. When a baby is born, it doesn't come out walking, talking, and well-educated. There is a process that causes all of these things. They exercise their senses. They exercise their vision, their ability to hear and discern sounds, etc. They exercise.

So you have all been born in the realm of the Spirit with everything you need to walk as a mature son or daughter. You have to exercise and learn to process things. I had to exercise, and so I understood the process. As the Lord began to take us down this path, giving me the revelation of Isaiah 60:8, I said, "Lord, are You saying what I think You are saying in this, as we understand this?"

The Lord said, "As you progress in this season and understand that you are beings of light, that you are really light, you will begin to do things that make physics irrelevant. You are a higher form of light than created light." Physics cannot figure out translocation. They say they could accomplish this with a photon of light, and they have actually done that in a lab. But to do that with mass? No, that doesn't work for them. Well, that's nothing to God.

Martin de Porres

Have you ever heard of Martin de Porres? He was a young man who served in a monastery in Peru in the 1600s. He was passionate for God, and the only outlet available for the knowledge of God at the time was the Catholic Church. But this young man would spend hours and days just praying and worshiping God. He was training as a 16-year-old to be a physician, but his passion was so much for God that he left that vocation and went into the monastery to serve the monks. They gave him a cell, or room where he would sleep, and he would worship God. And they would oftentimes have to come look for him when he wouldn't show up for different tasks that he was required to do. The monks would open the door to his cell, and he would be in there so lost in worship that he had levitated off the floor. He didn't even know it. "Oh! That's the devil," some say. No. the devil didn't invent anything except for sin. We need to understand that. If what was happening to him was sin, then Jesus going up in the clouds was sin, too. That doesn't compute. And Jesus said, "What I do you can do."

> *Very truly I tell you, whoever believes in me will do the works I have been doing, and they will do*

even greater things than these, because I am going to the Father (John 14:12 NIV).

There were reports of people seeing Martin all over the world because he would translocate and minister to people all over. Many times someone would take the arduous journey on ship that took almost a year traveling from Europe and back, and they would say, "Hey! We saw you in...." He would hush them and tell them not to say anything. One day they had a special bell made that came from Spain, and they were going to put it up in the bell tower. All the monks were pulling on a rope, trying to raise the bell into position, and all of a sudden it started to slip. Martin was looking on and saw their dilemma and he flew up and picked up the bell and put it in the bell tower.

> This is recorded history. Who are these that fly as a cloud? I said, "God, I'm in!"

Isaiah 60 Expanded

I want to give you an amplification of Isaiah 60, but this came through my own word studies. It is nothing you can buy on Amazon. This came from hours of study, taking apart the Hebrew language, using the tools that are easily available, and I am going to give you a different rendering of this verse. This will take you up a notch. Instead of "Arise and shine," He is saying:

Stand up, accomplish, confirm, and decree the day. The break of day, that moment when light overwhelms darkness, when light has been introduced to the world and reached maturity in you, and the splendor, the weight, the glory, and honor of the Lord now irradiates you.

See and consider the misery, the destruction, the sorrow, the wickedness, the ignorance, and death that will cover the earth and the impenetrable gloom the people. But God Himself will manifest on you, irradiating and exposing His light, His life, His character and makeup. His splendor, His weight, His glory, His honor will be visible and discerned as inhabiting you. (That's light.)

That will cause the masses, the heathen, the nations of the world to be drawn and come, desiring to be conversant with that brightness, that revelation of the Lord that is in you and upon you. Kings, royalty, heads of state, and leaders of every kind will come desiring to receive the light of the revelation now coming forth from you. (Now that is my kind of evangelism!)

They are all gathering around and assembling before you. They are coming to you—do you see them? Your sons, your grandsons, your great-grandsons, and everybody who is backslidden. All those whom you have nourished in the past are coming from remote and distant places—your daughters, granddaughters, and great-granddaughters are returning to receive the impartation of faith and trust.

So there will be a permanence of that revelatory character that they see in you. When that takes place, you will see and be utterly astounded at the overflow of joy that will flood all of you; your heart, your soul, your understanding will be awestricken, and your mental restrictions and your religious boxes will be broken. The scope of your understanding will be greatly enlarged because the masses and wealth of many peoples will suddenly turn to your favor. Those who have opposed you will be overturned, and the attitudes of those who have doubted you, and who you really are, and your integrity in God will utterly change as they are converted.

The wealth, the power, the efficient might of the nations will turn to you, resorting to you as their strength. Companies of laborers with their burden-bearers will cover your needs. The young, burdened with contention and gloom, will come. They of the covenant will bring you their gold and their sweet-smelling incense. All of these will come together publicly giving thanks and singing the praises and adorations of Yahuah. All these flocks who have been in darkness (we've talked about religious Christians) and gloom will gather and assemble around you.

At the same time, those who are strong and abundant with fruit will attend to your needs, ministering to every aspect of your life. With joy and pleasure will they come to offer sacrifices of praise, and I will embellish, vaunt, and beautify the family, My family whom I shall honor with majesty.

Hallelujah! Jesus! I can't tell you how many times I go over this, again and again, because what you focus on you will connect with. And when connection comes, activation takes place. His Word is life and light, so stay in His Word.

I have a good friend whom I have known for 35 or 36

years. He made this statement, and I have quoted this in many places: "A steady diet of FOX news or Communist News Network (CNN) will build nothing in you but fear, and doubt, and unbelief. But a steady diet of the Word will build life."

Our Magnificent Obsession

If you want to know things to come and you want to know things that are going on in the world, ask Holy Spirit. He said that He would do that for us. He said, "I'll show you things to come." Do you want to know who the next president will be? Ask the Holy Spirit. I'm not going to tell you, but He already told me, so I've been praying a lot more. Are we a people of the Word, or are we a people who have heard the Word? Are we followers of Jesus, or are we disciples of Jesus? There is a big difference.

To Which Group Do You Belong?

Followers

The masses followed Jesus, but they vanished like cockroaches in the light when anything went contrary. Most of them came to hear the nice words because it was the entertainment of the day. They had not heard anything like this before, and they came because they were hungry. What's for dinner today? Will

Are we followers of Jesus, or are we disciples of Jesus? There is a big difference.

there be free lunch again? But when tough times came, they disappeared. Even the disciples failed at the very end. That is a picture of the end of the age. The Lord said He will stop it before that happens again. Because at the end of the age, if it were possible, even the very elect, the disciples, will be deceived, so He is going to shorten the time. Thank God.

Disciples

Disciples are 24/7, 365 days a year. Followers are casual. Many of you, I'm sure, know Andre Ashby. Do what he says—make Jesus your magnificent obsession. The truth is that every one of us has lust in our life. Use the biblical lust to earnestly desire. There is a biblical application concerning lust. Earnestly desire spiritual gifts. That means to lust after, to pursue with passion, so we might as well redeem it. Make Him your magnificent obsession because He is about to do something in your life; He doesn't release a message like this for no reason! The time is too short for "church as usual" and for getting your ears tickled. He is doing something. He is releasing prophetic declaration through the preaching of the Word and for revelation of the deeper mysteries, and it is active in the lives of many.

Cameroon

We were in Cameroon about two years ago. It has never been my heart to go to Africa. I am not against African missions, but we had so many other things on our plate. I said, "Lord, I don't want to go; there is too much going on." We were traveling far too much at that time (I thought), and

I kept saying, "Lord, I am Your man. I will do whatever You say, but my flesh is weak, and I sure hate these airplanes. I am tired of wasting so much time on an airplane. Will You please activate this translation by faith on a greater scale?" You know—Phillip Airlines.

Every African church we have been in, even in other countries, is boisterous, and their worship is just over the top. I love their worship. But we were invited to go to a movement that was prim and proper. They said, "We wear ties, we don't say amen, we sit down and take notes. And we definitely don't get demonstrative in worship."

Is this funny or what? God has got a sense of humor. Anyway, we went. Let me just say that they are not prim and proper anymore. God blew that place up! On the platform on the second day, I turned and I prophesied over a young lady there. I said, "You are going to be translated frequently now, understand that." I didn't remember this, but they told me afterward.

When we came back to the States, we started getting all sorts of testimonies. The young girl I prophesied over from that day on started having translocation experiences every day. Finally, she got to the point of saying, "God is this real? Is this really real?" The next day after praying that prayer, she was taken to a lake, somewhere quite distant from where she lived. She saw in the middle of the lake a little boy drowning, and she couldn't swim. She said, "Lord, help him."

And the Lord said, "No, you walk out there."

So she started walking and she walked across the lake. But by the time she got to where the boy was, he was dead, so she picked him up and she said, "Lord, what do I do?"

The Lord said, "Take him and place him under the tree," and so she did and suddenly she was back in the room,

The Lord had told her that it was the boy's time to come home. That evening on the news, on live broadcast, they showed the boy's family who had found his drowned body lying there under the tree. The mother came on, weeping and saying, "Whoever rescued my son's body from the lake, I want to thank you. Now we can have closure." She realized then that this was real and she goes every day.

As you read some of these accounts, I realize that this is "tweaking" you a bit. I share and teach these things to provoke you. I am not doing this to give you just some nice message, with three main points and a poem. This is life to me. Taking His Word and believing it and living it—that is how we choose to live. God is saying that He wants a people who will believe Him about the progression of light and that God is light. In Him is no darkness. Jesus was the light of the world and He still is, but He is the light of the world in you. Let your light so shine before men.

How many realize that there is a different connotation concerning "light" in the Word? We used to think it was good deeds, good works—you know, light. That is light too. It is love, it is a generous heart, it is the character of Christ, it is all these things, but there is a different element being applied to it today because people will actually see the manifestation of light. You will be a glowing one, literally. It is the Mount of Transfiguration in combat boots right now. They are going to see this upon us, just as they saw Moses who had to put a veil over himself. That was a lesser covenant, and in this new covenant, when Jesus came down off of the Mount of Transfiguration, it says in Mark 9:15, they ran to Him in astonishment—like wow!

Why did that happen? Because He was still glowing. He made a choice to ratchet that down at the time because it was for a generation yet to come. There were three disciples who saw it, and they were Peter, James, and John. They were the only three who ever expressed it or talked about it in the New Covenant. They were looking for it because they knew it was a sign of the end of the age.

It was called "the perusia." When Christ who is our life shall appear, we will appear as like Him because we will see Him as He is (see 1 John 3:2). There are two different words here. There is perusia and phaneroo. Perusia means "when He presences Himself together with us." There is a measure of intimacy here. In the classical Greek, when an emperor was on a journey into a far country and he was tired of traveling for days and weeks, he would decide, "Hey, there is Apostle Jim's house. I am going to go hang out with him for a while just to rest." That was called a "presencing" or perusia. Then a phaneroo

> In this process, because we are seeing Him, we are going to start becoming like Him, and He is light.

is an open manifestation. So those two words combined express what happens before the catching away.

We always interpreted this verse as being about His appearing when He comes back for us. That's not correct—this is prior to that. There is a progression here, and if you study this in the Greek it says that He is going to progressively increase in His interaction with His people through visitation and open manifestation before He comes and says, "Come home!" And in this process, because we are seeing Him, we are going to start becoming like Him, and He is light.

> *Dear friends, now we are children of God, and what we will be has not yet been made known. But we know that when Christ appears, we shall be like him, for we shall see him as he is (1 John 3:2 NIV).*

Christ-like

Let me give you a word of caution. Because it is the flavor of the day, many people are coming out with testimonies of "Oh! I have been in Heaven, and you know, I did this and that and the other thing." Let me tell you something—if you don't see the fruit of a changed life, meaning greater holiness in that life, do not believe it. Don't believe it at all. It is time we look past the giftings and experiences to character and to the fruit of the Spirit being evident, because if you have a genuine encounter with the King of Glory, you can't help but be changed into that image. It is the same thing with gifting. I don't care how gifted anybody is; if I don't see the fruit of character and of righteousness, I shy away.

The gifts are real. They can be genuine, but they can also be false. But I don't want to be smeared with a mixture. Pay attention to what God is actually saying. Stop chasing after gifts and start chasing Jesus and the gifts will follow you. Manifestations, signs, wonders, and miracles will happen. They happen because you are pursuing Him. It is all about the pursuit of Jesus, and the more you pursue Him, the more you become like Him.

Now look at Moses and the pillar of fire. I love this story because I have experienced it. The Lord has shown Himself in the pillar of cloud and the pillar of fire, and it is an interesting study, but in the Hebrew, the Shekinah glory of God is the reddish-gold coloring of the presence of God that manifested to the children of Israel. Shekinah is not a word in Scripture. It is something the rabbis came up with to try and describe this experience of the pillar of cloud and pillar of fire. It comes from a Hebrew root word, shakenn, which means to dwell together as neighbors in friendship and intimacy.

The Shekinah Glory

The Shekinah glory of God is for those who are in intimate friendship with God. To the unredeemed flesh, it means the terror of Yahweh. Do you know that Pharaoh and his people could have overtaken the children of Israel within hours? If you start hiking with two million people with all of their cattle and children, you can be sure that mob barely moved. Maybe they covered five miles a day because a crowd that large moves with the accordion effect, and it just isn't very fast. They might have been two or three days out. That's only a couple of hours by chariot. What kept them, then, from connecting with the children of Israel? It was the pillar of fire. It was terror to unsanctified human flesh.

The fear of God kept the Egyptians away, but on the other side, to those in covenant with God, it was a wooing and a drawing. It was like Daddy saying, "Come here, kids! Let me hug you." That's the difference. To the redeemed, it is the love of God. To the unredeemed, it is the terror of God. Because flesh (that which is unholy) cannot abide in the presence of the living God.

Flesh (that which is unholy) cannot abide in the presence of the living God.

If you are light, what happens to those enemies of the cross? Persecution is coming, let me tell you that. Persecution is coming, it is already slowly rearing its head in America. But when you become the glowing ones, they run from you in terror. Unfortunately, it is not the whole Church. But there is going to be a forerunner company of believers. I am telling you that you don't mess with God's glory. It won't happen. It can't happen. It is diametrically opposed and impossible because that which is not life cannot touch the glory without being consumed.

Here is my experience with this pillar of fire. Some years ago in Kirkland, Washington, where Microsoft is located, there was a revival going on for months and they asked me if I would come and minister there. The fear of God grabbed my heart. I knew I didn't want my flesh to step into a place like that and quell and quench the flow of the Spirit of God, so I began to fast and pray. I had never been able to fast before that for more than three days, but this was easy. The fear of God made it real simple. I fasted seven days straight, and then I went up. The worship there went on for two or three hours, and it was awesome. Intercession went on 24/7 in that place, as they would walk back and forth.

Pillar of Fire

On the second day there, I was lost in worship and it was quite loud there. I had worked at Boeing in Seattle at one point for about 18 months and they have an APU, an auxiliary power unit, that they would put in the back of the jet aircraft, and that was what would crank up the engines.

I opened my eyes to see what was going on, and there was a pillar of fire on the platform.

They were really loud. So at this place, I was in worship, and all of a sudden I was hearing this incredible flame-like sound of a jet engine. I thought, "What in the world is that?" I knew we were not by an airport. I opened my eyes to see what was going on, and there was a pillar of fire on the platform.

I heard it and I saw it, and I was completely awestruck! I have to tell the truth. Back then I was a little more relaxed in my approach to things. I am kind of quirky and I have got my mother's sense of humor. I had two or three friends with me, and so I said, "Hey! John! Go up by the platform." People had been dancing, but they had moved. He asked why. I said, "God is up there."

He said, "OK" and he went up there and bam! He dropped like sack of potatoes.

So I said, "Hey! Roy! Go up by the platform. God is there." He went, and bam, he fell. Pastor Jerry, the third guy I sent up, dropped too!

I was thinking about the senior pastor. I wondered how he would feel about this. I thought, "I don't even have to minister tonight because he can't get up there to introduce me." I thought that idea sounded pretty good, and I just watched all this in awe.

Then, the pastor came up to me and said, "Look, I am not going to introduce you tonight, just go up there."

Thinking about the fire of God up there on the platform, I said, "That's not funny, God." He had been teaching me, and He still teaches me how to move in Him.

Learn to Stand

God said, "I want you to learn how to stand in the "kabod" of God, the weighty glory, because the hour is coming when if you haven't exercised yourself to be able to stand, you won't be able to be effective in ministry." I had been practicing, but I had never experienced anything quite like this before.

There were only four steps up to the platform, but I think

I crawled there on my lips—I don't really know. I was hanging on for dear life, and the Lord said, "Prophesy to the pastor."

I said, "Pastor, I've got a word for you," and in response he started walking up. I said, "No, stay there!" But when I started prophesying to him, he went flying back four rows and dropped to the ground also!

I don't remember the rest of the night. I don't even know how I got off the platform. The next day we were five miles away, and I began to hear that sound again, and I looked into the distance, and there again was the pillar of fire. I was completely undone. Do you know what the Lord is saying in this? He is saying that this is going to become a common manifestation for us in this hour, a supernatural common manifestation. I mean that.

It changed my life because there is still flesh in me. I still deal with things like everybody does, but that was a major flash-burn. It was poof, and I got set free of some things; I was like a bug in a bug light. I tell everybody, everywhere I go, that in my life the Lord has had a great sense of humor with me. He loves to joke with me. He is always kidding with me. If you don't believe the Lord has a sense of humor, look at the people in your life.

You've heard about the gemstones that fall from Heaven and stuff like that? I was ministering in Fiji, and there was about a 40-foot ceiling in the place where we were ministering. I was teaching away, and as I read my text from the script, I stood up and plop—right on the Bible fell two geckos. And they kind of composed themselves and ran off, and I said, "Yeah right, God! Everybody else gets gemstones and I get geckos!" Everybody just rolled in laughter.

I was ministering in Malaysia for a week straight at the FGA, the Full Gospel Assembly, one of the largest churches in Malaysia. About the third night, I was looking across the auditorium, and I saw this huge thing floating down, and I thought, "Is that a feather? No, it can't be." So right in the middle of things, I said, "Excuse me, is that a feather?"

And a lady responded, "No, it's dust from the air conditioner."

That's the Lord's sense of humor toward me. So you see, I do get the unusual manifestations that most people don't get—namely, geckos and dust. God does things like that with me. That is my relationship with God.

9

STEPPING INTO THE GLORY

Moses said to the Lord, "You have been telling me, 'Lead these people,' but you have not let me know whom you will send with me. You have said, 'I know you by name and you have found favor with me.' If you are pleased with me, teach me your ways so I may know you and continue to find favor with you. Remember that this nation is your people."

The Lord replied, "My Presence will go with you, and I will give you rest."

Then Moses said to him, "If your Presence does not go with us, do not send us up from here. How will anyone know that you are pleased with me and with your people unless you go with us? What else will distinguish me and your people from all the other people on the face of the earth?"

> The more I learn, the less I know, and the hungrier I get. Because He is too vast.

And the Lord said to Moses, "I will do the very thing you have asked, because I am pleased with you and I know you by name."

Then Moses said, "Now show me your glory" (Exodus 33:12-18 NIV).

Show Me Your Glory

This is the story of Moses, who said, "Lord, I want to see Your glory." I want to bring you into the amplification—the word study. We are going to break it down just a little bit. This is what Moses is saying to the Lord. Essentially, he is saying, "Lord, You say that You know me, but I don't really know You." That is a truthful saying for every one of us. As much as you know, you don't know. As a matter of fact, some time ago, the Lord gave me this—the more I learn, the less I know, and the hungrier I get. Because He is too vast.

So here is what He would say in the amplification, the word study:

"Now, if You would, Lord, I beg of You, if I have found favor and acceptance in how You see me, reveal to me Your innermost thoughts and heart's desires. Help me to see what You see and to know the path You have set for me and for this nation. My desire is to become pleasing to You, to find complete acceptance with You. Let's not forget that Israel, this nation, is Your chosen nation and people."

And the Lord said, "The face of My visible presence will proceed you and accompany you, and I will cause you to be at peace and breathe easily."

I like that. And Moses responded:

"If the face of Your visible presence (the key being visible) does not proceed and accompany us, then do not lead or take us to that land. Because how else is it going to be known among the nations that I, as the leader, and this nation, as Your people, have found favor and acceptance with You?"

I said, "Lord, if that is the measure of favor and acceptance, then most of us are way outside the camp." Even so, my prayer was, "Lord, this is what I want."

He responded, "It is Isaiah 60 time. This is what you will get." Moses continued:

"Won't it be because You precede us and accompany us that they know? By this means we will be regarded as distinguished and set apart. I and this nation as Your people from every other tribe, nation, and people spread across the face of the earth."

And the Lord answered and declared to Moses, "Now listen to this: I will perform this word exactly as you have requested."

When has God ever said that to you? I've already told you that I have given Him some tremendous suggestions. He has never taken me up on any of them. But you see, this request came from a leader's heart, and it wasn't about "look at me," it was about "remember Your covenant with Your people." So God said He would perform the Word exactly as Moses requested and required, for he had indeed found favor and acceptance with Him, and He knew Moses' character, his makeup, his honor and trustworthiness, and his integrity. That is why he received from God.

"Then, Lord, if You will, reveal to me and allow me to experience Your glory," and He answered, "I will cause the entirety of Myself, My Kingdom, My fairness, My beauty,

My joy, My prosperity, My goodness, and My discernment to transition in phases by and upon you.

I will address and pronounce the nature, the character, the makeup, the personality of YodHehVavHeh, Yahweh, to you personally. I will demonstrate to you that I bestow favor, and acceptance, and mercy on whom I choose to show My love, favor, acceptance, and mercy. That is you. You cannot see My face or see into My eyes because it is not possible for any person of the Adamic seed to see and experience My face, or see into Me and live, or continue in life.

But since Jesus died and shed His blood, we are no longer Adamic seed according to the Book of Colossians. He replaced our Adamic DNA with His DNA. That is how it reads in the Aramaic. So now we can see Him face to face. And the Lord, continuing His promise, said:

Watch! Pay attention now! There is a space here next to Me where I will station you and have you stand on a cliff—a place of faith. At the same time, when My glory moves and transitions past you, I will place you in the crevice in the rock and screen you in, covering and overshadowing you with the hollow of My hand while I pass by. But as soon as I pass by, I will remove My hand, which has been covering you, and you will get to see all that I have done, all of time past from the beginning of creation up to the present, but you will not get to see and experience My face or see into My eyes or know Me that way.

The Invasion of Heaven

We have muddled around for over 2,000 years. We are not getting too far on our own, so there is an invasion of Heaven on earth that is about to take that which is unattainable, even though you have a passion for it, and make it reality.

This is why Moses was able to write the book of Genesis. He saw everything from the creation to that moment. That's the glory—there is no time; there is no space. There is no past, present, or future in God's light and God's glory; it is all now with God. I want to encourage you with this fact. God is releasing a new dispensation of maturity in the Church. It is a sovereign act of God because none of us will get there on our own. We can't, and we have muddled around for over 2,000 years. We are not getting too far on our own, so there is an invasion of Heaven on earth that is about to take that which is unattainable, even though you have a passion for it, and make it reality. It is going to be sovereign. You are not going to figure this out; you are not going to make it happen. The only thing you can do is agree with the Word of God and say, "Yes, Lord, I am available. I desire to be made like You."

Remember the praying prodigal. He went from give me to make me. This is the season of, "Lord, make me." All it takes is an agreement. It is the easiest, most difficult thing you will ever do. Why? Because you have to shut off the stinkin' thinkin' and get back to the Word. All things are possible if somebody believes? No. All things are possible to you if you believe. It is no longer the day of "be it done unto you according to the pastor's faith." It has got to be according to your faith. We have placed the burden of the Church far too long on the shoulders of pastors and those who have been set as shepherds to tend sheep, and it is not going to work anymore.

It is time for the Body of Christ to arise. That means you have to engage the Kingdom of Heaven by faith and not passively watch it go by and just wish. Jump into the mix. The Lord told me this several years ago: "I would rather see you err in faith than succeed in doubt." So when I take a step of faith, if I make a mistake He says, "It is OK, you tried, you are blessed. Now let Me correct the direction." But if I stand there and doubt, it breaks His heart. So if you step out in faith and you miss the mark, you have stepped out in faith and God honors that.

Steps of Faith

You will never be a success without failures. It's impossible! Why do we fear failure? Because we don't like to look foolish. Well, it is already too late! You look foolish. We have all looked foolish to somebody, and we will again. Who cares about that? We should want to look righteous and pleasing in the eyes of God. So I would like you to do something by faith.

Here is what I want you to do. I want you to find a bag of some sort, and as a prophetic gesture I want you to reach into that bag and see something.

When you reach into the bag, believe God will show you something in your thoughts or imagination. As He shows you something in your sanctified imagination, reach around in the bag and believe for it to be manifest in this natural realm.

I have expectations for you because God has promised me that it is going to become tangible. I am believing for tangible. I mean tangible where you can say, "Look at that!" Tangible like a gemstone. But also, don't be hung up on tangible. Do this by faith, because there will be an impact in your life. It will change.

In our conference two years ago, we had Brother Sadhu Sundar Selvaraj there, and I saw two things that I had to do. One of the times that I have been in Heaven, God gave me a chalice by a river of revelation that is an offshoot of the River of Life. When I had taken of that, it was like a continuous download of revelation. I said, "Lord, how am I supposed to remember all this?"

He said, "You don't have to remember that, it is now part of you." Revelation began to flow out of my life, so I saw myself taking that chalice and handing it to somebody in the conference, and they were to drink from it. And then I also saw a softball-sized ruby.

You have got to understand this about a ruby. A ruby speaks of the blood of Jesus and the fire of God. Because of the structure of the atoms in a ruby, it refracts light in such a way as to create heat. The first visible laser was created by bouncing light through a ruby. I don't know why it works, but it does. So it speaks of the blood of Jesus, and it speaks of covenant; it speaks also of the fire of God. There is an aspect of revelation in life, too.

I said, "Lord, no, I won't." I was reasoning to myself, "This guy has these experiences all the time!" God didn't answer that. I have some powerful advice for you. When Heaven gets quiet, just do what He told you to do. So I came up and I said, "OK, I am just going to do my prophetic thing." I reached in and grabbed the chalice and I said, "Who do I give it too, Lord?"

I saw the chalice, and the Lord said to me, "You are going to take this and give it to someone else."

And the Lord said, "Give it to Brother Sadhu." And he came forward and my worship leader stood behind him as a catcher.

I said, "Oh, that's faith! I like this!" He just made the gesture of drinking from that chalice, and they both got drunk. They were falling down drunk! And I thought, "I knew that would happen!" Now this was a stretch for me, but I continued and said, "Brother Sadhu, this is what I see." The gracious man that he is, he just took the chalice from me and stood there for a minute and sat down, and then I continued on.

At the end of the meeting I went down into the audience and he asked to go back to his room. I thought, "Oh, man! I must have really stepped in this." Reshma and I both were thinking, "Dear God, what happened?" I thought I must have offended him.

We took him back to his room, and the next day he came back, and I asked, "Is everything OK?"

He said, "Brother, you don't know what that did for me," and he began to tell us about the breakthrough that came for him. He said, "When that breakthrough came to me last night, I was visited. I was in the council of Heaven, and they said to me, 'Tell Bruce that the day is coming when he is going to reach in and take forth scrolls with revelation.'"

What a powerful word from the Lord that came from following the Lord's instruction of a prophetic gesture! Yes, God is doing this in this hour! Be encouraged! Seek Him and His righteousness. He is going to use you in ways beyond your wildest imaginations!

A Prayer

Father, by faith I am reaching into the portal. I am bringing forth out of the realm of the third heaven into the natural realm those things you had me gather and collect in the third heaven. Father, I distribute them now as You have told me to. And I thank You, Father, for an impartation of revelation, and of light and life into their mortal bodies, and I thank You for it in Jesus' name. Amen.

I just release this now to everyone who is reading this book and will receive this revelation. Let it be unto you according to your faith.

The Word of the Lord

"I also release to you that which you have not asked. There are blessings that have been reserved for this generation, and I decree that these blessings are now beginning to flow in your life. Eyes are now being opened so that your spiritual sight will be acute. Ears are being fine tuned so that you know My voice with great clarity. Hearts are being repositioned to beat in synch with My heart. Understanding is now coming, and you're going to be able to walk in this hour with greater purpose and clarity than you have ever known. Right now I release to you the promise for your family. I have told you in Acts 16:31 if you believed, you shall be saved, and your family. Watch and see what My covenant promise can accomplish now in your family. Because you have believed, I am increasing in you, and I will cause your ability to step out in faith to increase. There is a measure of the gift of faith being released in each one of you this night. And that which has been difficult to grasp hold of by faith is now going to seem easy, and you are going to set your sights to even greater things in the realm of the Spirit and in the Kingdom of Heaven, because your faith is increasing this night. I am pleased to see a people who are willing to look foolish in the eyes of man and stand forth in faith before Me. Because you have pleased Me and blessed Me, I am going to bless you."

A Final Word!

Hallelujah! I receive that, Father. This is a blessing from me: "Lord, give them all geckos." Hallelujah!

Lord, give them all geckos

About the Author

Dr. Bruce Allen is an internationally known minister of the gospel of Jesus Christ, keynote conference speaker, and author of several books, including the bestseller Gazing into Glory. Bruce ministers from the glory realms of God with miracles and signs following. A modern-day Enoch, Bruce's mandate from the Lord Jesus is to train and equip believers in the supernatural things of God, to live a life of miracles, signs, and wonders, moving supernaturally across the earth for the purposes of and the glory of the Lord. It is Dr. Bruce's passion to bring believers into their full inheritance in Christ.

Dr. Bruce is also the founder of Still Waters International Ministries, a guest on It's Supernatural! with Sid Roth, and the host of the popular television program For His Glory on Angel TV.

www.stillwatersinternationalministries.com

OTHER BOOKS FROM BRUCE ALLEN

Bruce Allen books are available at Still Waters International Ministries or at bookstores and book distributors worldwide.

www.stillwatersinternationalministries.com

Made in the USA
Columbia, SC
28 August 2019